ADHD 101

A Guidebook for Parents

Greg M. Romaneck & Derek Harkema

Bloomington, IN 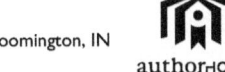 Milton Keynes, UK

authorHOUSE®

AuthorHouse™
1663 Liberty Drive, Suite 200
Bloomington, IN 47403
www.authorhouse.com
Phone: 1-800-839-8640

AuthorHouse™ UK Ltd.
500 Avebury Boulevard
Central Milton Keynes, MK9 2BE
www.authorhouse.co.uk
Phone: 08001974150

First published by AuthorHouse 2/19/2007

ISBN: 978-1-4259-8652-0 (sc)

Printed in the United States of America
Bloomington, Indiana

This book is printed on acid-free paper.

Cover Art by Erin Elizabeth Romaneck
Cover Design by Kyle M. Romaneck

DEDICATION

The authors of this small booklet would like to dedicate their work to their family members. In a society where so many pressures are exerted to break down the nourishing elements of families it is only through the love of such wonderful people that accomplishments can be made. We both want to acknowledge our families for all the love, encouragement, support, and kindness you have shown us. Hopefully, we have been worthy of such care and decency.

DH/GMR
1/2007

TABLE OF CONTENTS

1.

Introduction: Why Read This Booklet?

Every year more and more youngsters in the United States and other nations are identified with Attention Deficit Disorder (ADD). For many of those children & adolescents the years leading up to a correct diagnosis and treatment have been marked by school failure, family conflict, poor social relationships, and sadness. ADD is a medical syndrome that causes youngsters and adults to:

- Lack focus
- Struggle with multi-step directions
- Demonstrate inconsistent learning
- Show limited social skills
- Under perform at work & school
- Generate stress and anxiety in themselves and loved ones
- Behave impulsively
- Make critical errors in judgment
- Experience other mental health issues such as depression & anxiety.
- Experiment with forms of self-medication like alcohol and drugs
- Wonder if life is worth living

ADD is an immensely disruptive mental health disorder that manifests itself in ways that can fundamentally alter a person's life. One National Institutes of Health publication describes ADD as "living in a fast-moving kaleidoscope, where sounds, images, and thoughts are constantly shifting (Kuhar, Candle, & Little 113). In many cases when asked why they did something that was obviously not in anyone best interest a youngster with ADD may well say, "I really don't know."

In terms of symptoms ADD impacts people in different ways at different ages. In infancy, a child destined to manifest ADD symptoms may be very wakeful and cry a great deal. Such young children may appear to constantly have colic and are very demanding of attention from their caregivers but then remain unable to be soothed. Elementary-aged children may be disruptive in school, restless, aggressive, sullen, withdrawn, or always on the go. At school or at home such youngsters may seem to "always have their engines running." By adolescence an undiagnosed youngster may demonstrate more risk-taking behaviors, might be at high risk of school dropout, or may be in constant trouble at home or in the community.

While many of the behaviors above may occur in youngsters not having ADD, in a person with the syndrome they will remain in place and may well worsen over time without intervention. However, in order to be identified as having ADD rigorous examination is needed.

One of the great criticisms of the increase in ADD diagnosis in recent years has been that anyone and everyone who is assessed by professionals ends up being identified as having ADD. In order to accurately diagnose ADD a medical or mental health professional should apply standards drawn from the Psychiatric Associations

Diagnostic and Statistical Manual of Mental Disorders (DSM). The DSM definition of ADD requires that a client's symptoms to be long term, excessive, and highly disruptive to life functioning. The client's behaviors must also be so severe that they impact upon the person's life in a way that is meaningful. For example, a child whose disruptive actions in the classroom cause some school problems but who can change the way they act is not ADD. Conversely, a youngster who acts in an unpredictably impulsive manner at school, at home, and in the community and whose life is negatively affected in all settings may well be ADD.

Another factor to keep in mind about ADD is that the symptoms must occur in at least two important settings. For example, a child who demonstrates poor concentration at school but who is attentive at church, in the home, on the job, and in clubs is probably not ADD. Issues of potential learning disability, a mismatch with the teacher's style, or other concerns may be operating but probably not ADD.

Nationally, current research varies but approximately 3-5% of the population may have ADD. Some experts feel that this percentage is far below what really exists due to the inability of many families to either recognize the sources of their children's problems or a lack of financial and other resources needed to facilitate a proper assessment. In the United States up to three million school-aged children and adolescents—at least one per classroom nationwide—are thought to be have ADD. Within this population of children males are far more likely to be identified as having ADD than females. Though statistics vary according to different surveys the ratio of boys to girls diagnosed as having ADD ranges from around 2:1 to as high as 9:1.

Over the years ADD has gone under a variety of labels. In the past, prior to the full recognition of the term ADD, many youngsters who suffered from this disorder went undiagnosed. Those children and teens were simply seen as "trouble makers" "delinquents," "antsy," or any number of other descriptors. Then, once researchers began to look into the origins of children's behaviors with greater care, terms such as hyperkinesis, hyperkinesias disorder, minimal brain dysfunction minimal neurological disorder, and hyperactivity were all used. In more recent years the term Attention Deficit Disorder with Hyperactivity (ADHD) was the preferred term. In this booklet the terms ADD & ADHD are used interchangeably although there certainly are differences between active and passive versions of this syndrome.

The diagnosis of ADD is a sometimes controversial subject. From the perspective of many school officials, many ADD diagnoses are suspect. Teachers, school administrators, and other support staff often look at assessments done by medical or mental health professionals that are disconnected from the child's life in school. In those instances, a child's ADD diagnosis may be questioned by school representatives who then doubt the entire field of ADD research. Thus, when having your child assessed for potential ADD it is important to realize that the more comprehensive the evaluation is, and the more involved school staff are in providing information to the assessors, the greater the "buy-in" your child's teachers will have in the entire process.

School can be one of the prime areas where children and youths with ADD demonstrate both their symptoms and the negative results of them. Without being sarcastic it can be very easy for children with ADD to develop a menu of school-based problems that will leave parents and school officials pulling their hair out. Indeed, many parents of children with ADD can hardly break a sweat and still create a list of issues their son or daughter has created at school. In fact, the list below may be familiar to you if you have a child that has or who you think might have ADD:

Common Ways to Guarantee School Failure if you are ADD or Undiagnosed ADD

- Never do homework or even know it has been assigned

- Always leave your books either at home or in your locker

- Never study for a test until it is too late to pass

- Always have your hand up in class and wave it around

- Ignore teachers when they ask you to do things

- Blurt out answers to a point where your teach hates you

- Never listen to the vice principal when he or she tells you something

- Make sure the PE teachers or coaches see you as a pain in the butt

- Have the messiest desk your teacher has ever seen

- Make sure that the homework that should take thirty minutes lasts for three hours

- Always fight with your parents about any school assignments

- Bring home report cards peppered with "F's" even though you have "A" knowledge

- Forget every assignment, detention, or project until the time to turn it in or serve it has passed

- Develop a reputation as the class clown

- Question school authorities without thinking about the power they might have

- Get 100% on this week's spelling test and 10% next week

- Irritate virtually every other kid in class because you act without thinking

- Do anything to impress other kids so you can have "friends"

- Answer teacher's questions about your behavior by saying "I don't know"

- Tell teachers they are stupid or answer "Whatever" when they tell you your life is a failure

- Always forget your pencil and remind the teacher of that fact

While this list is far from comprehensive, many of the items included in it are typical of the sorts of problems students with ADD experience and create in schools every day of their lives. Over time, if they are untreated and misunderstood, these types of behaviors will result in:

1. School failure

2. Terrible self-esteem

3. Animosity on the part of school staff toward your child

4. Poor social judgment

5. General problems

6. Issues that will transfer into adult failures

While there are no definitive causes of ADD various risk factors have been identified by researchers. ADD tends to run in families. Birth complications can be a factor that influences neurological development and may be part of a child's ADD profile. Neurological differences in people with ADD and those without have been identified in some cases. In those circumstances appropriate medication can be a valuable part of a person's treatment plan. Poor parenting is generally no longer thought to be a major contributor to ADD. In general, ADD is believed to be a medical condition caused by internal differences in children who process information and neurologically function in ways that affect their behavior, concentration, and actions.

A major fear that many parents of children with ADD or who are suspected of having ADD express is that of future substance abuse if medication is used as part of treatment. Recent studies indicate that up to 50% of individuals identified as having ADD who do not use medication as part of their treatment will abuse substances. In those studies youngsters with ADD who are untreated medically are "much more likely to become substance abusers" and their abuse is "likely to start earlier in life, last longer, and have less chance of mitigation." (Kuhar, Candle & Little 115)

In looking at these sorts of statistics it is possible to come to the conclusion that the failure to consider appropriate medication for a child legitimately suffering from ADD can be one that is understandable but that also has long-term consequences. Conversely, medical research as to the long-term side effects of medication usage aimed at controlling ADD is inconclusive. There are many side effects that medications prescribed to treat ADD create. Those side effects can be disturbing and hurtful and are a major source of parental opposition to the use of stimulants and other medications. However, what can be said is that much of the creditable research about the treatment of ADD emphasizes using all the available tools to help the child inclusive of counseling, family involvement, medical supports, and close communication between home & school.

In terms of the use of this particular booklet the authors hope that a few goals can be achieved. This booklet was designed to offer parents of youngsters with ADD another tool in their efforts to help their children. Both authors have children of their own who have been diagnosed with ADD. In their own lives problems at school, in the home, and within the community related to their children's disabilities have helped them to understand the issues faced by other parents of children with ADD. Therefore, this is not a publication designed to market a particular "magical" approach to ADD. There are no commercials touting a particular counseling philosophy or medication treatment. Likewise, both authors have worked in or with school systems for a combined total of over forty years. Both of the authors of this pamphlet realize the issues faced by both parents and school officials when it comes to appropriately educating a child with ADD. However, this experience has not led either writer to believe that any child's education is "hopeless" because of their ADD. NO, all children can learn and generally most people involved in their education can at least be led to the same conclusion.

This booklet is aimed at providing parents practical suggestions in areas of importance. For example, if this publication serves its purpose you should be able to have at least some information designed to help you answer question like:

- How can I pick a counselor for my child?
- What rights does my child have in school?
- What's the difference between an IEP and a 504 Plan?
- What are the pros and cons of medication?
- How can I discipline my child?
- Is my child lazy or just in need of help?
- What can I do to control my temper when my child is driving me nuts?
- Why is there so much stress in my family?
- Is it OK to question my own parenting skills?

- How come my child always knows what buttons to push when we argue?

- How can I make sure my child's school meeting goes well?

- Is it OK to let my child fail sometimes?

- How can I make sure other people understand my child's needs?

- Who can I turn to for more information or help regarding ADD?

- Are there other books I should read?

- Am I to blame for my child's behaviors?

Being a parent is the hardest job in the world. There is no end to your shift at work when it comes to parenthood. Likewise, you cannot "retire" from parenthood. No, once you are a parent you have guaranteed lifetime employment as such. On the other hand, what is more important than being a good parent? Can you imagine something that is more valuable than the time you dedicate to your child's welfare? If you can, then you really need to step back and question your own attitudes about your children. This little booklet has grown out of our experiences as parents and professionals. It is designed to provide you, the reader, with food for thought about being the parent of a child with ADD. Hopefully, you will come away from this booklet with at least one idea that made you reflect about how you love, nurture, relate to, and handle your own child. If so, then the authors have achieved their humble purpose and made use of their modest talents. If not, please feel free to make use of the email addresses provided in the resources section of this publication to let us know how we can improve our work and better assist parents.

Good luck in your journey as a parent and we wish you well in your efforts.

SOURCE

Kuhar, Michael J., Candler, Charles Howard, & Liddle, Howard (ed.). *Drugs and Society (3 Vol.'s)*. New York, NY: Marshall Cavendish, 2006.

2.

Social Skills:

The Building Blocks to Lifetime Happiness

One area that children with ADD often show deficits in is that of social skills. But, should that be so surprising? Imagine a person who is bright and capable but who often blurts out answers in game situations, has difficulty paying attention when you are talking to them, frequently jumps around in conversations, acts impulsively, takes unnecessary risks, does anything to get attention, and always has their motor running. How much time would you like to spend with a person like that? If your answer is, "Not very much," then you have the beginnings of an understanding of why people with ADD often struggle in social situations.

The ability to regulate your behavior in a socially acceptable manner has many applications. In life, relationships are often the seat of much of our happiness. If you are limited in terms of your social skills you may well be limited in regards to establishing successful relationships. To succeed in work requires knowledge and "know how" but also the capacity for following directions, arriving on time, working well with others, and reading the nuances of people's behavior. Thus, in most of the major sectors of a person's life their ability to use reasonable social skills is one of the most important sources of success and happiness they can possibly possess. Sadly, children, adolescents, and adults with

ADD often have shortcomings in this vital area of human behavior.

How can loving adults help children with ADD hone their social skills? Are there ways in which people with ADD can learn improved social skills? Is it simply a lost cause and will a person with ADD just have to accept their isolation or social failures as their lot in life? What follows are suggestions and frameworks that may shed some light on ways in which people with ADD can improve and regulate their social behavior. Hopefully, some of these tips will ring true with you and the people in your life who have ADD.

A. **At a very young age engage the child in as many positive activities as possible:** If you can engage a child with ADD in activities you may help him or her to discover what some of their strengths and interests are. Through sports, clubs, organizations, study groups, church or community organizations, and family activities a child with ADD can come to see themselves as competent or outstanding in avenues that they might otherwise never have experienced. For example, your son may prove to be an amazingly talented singer who can maintain his attention all through the choir performances at church and school. In that ability rests not only a musical accomplishment but also a source of respect from others, and a buffering of the fact that he may struggle in other aspects of his life. Help your son or daughter to discover their talents and then encourage those talents, as a loving parent should.

B. **Stress thinking & feeling:** When your son or daughter comes to you in pain because they have been rejected or they think they have failed do not simply dismiss them or say, "Oh, you'll get over it. Everybody fails at something." While it certainly may be true that everyone fails at something, that knowledge will do virtually nothing to assuage your child's pain. In fact, your effort at minimizing your child's hurt may leave them with the impression that you, just like everybody else, simply does not care about them. If you see your child in pain talk to them, listen, and act out of love. If you can model thinking and feeling in your family you give your child the gift of sensitivity. Over time, this sort of modeling can help them to become more sensitive themselves as parents, friends, co-workers, or any number of future roles. When we act as loving and reasonable beings we offer the best of ourselves to a child who we cherish but who struggles to feel successful & proficient.

C. **Practice conversation skills:** Tired as you may be, take time to converse with your children. Find topics that they are interested in and listen to them tell you about them. If they get stuck in a long-winded monologue about anime cartoon shows, video games, or sports politely remind them that it is a conversation and not a speech. Practice turn taking and emphasize that you are interested in what they have to say. Remember the Taoist saying, "Am I listening, or merely waiting to speak." Value your child enough to give them the gift of time to tell you about what they think is important. If your child can show improvement in his or her ability to converse within the family, they certainly can demonstrate that same growth in public.

D. **Teach and model good listening skills:** Sometimes one of the hardest things for parents to do is listen to their children. The world is a very complicated place. Jobs, money problems, world events, and any number of other distractions can draw our attention away from the members of our family. That is why it is so important to take time to listen to your children when they speak to you. If, when your daughter begins to tell you about her day at school, your mind is still back at the office, she might as well be a ghost for all the reality you see in her words and presence. When we actively listen we share in another person's world. Through encouraging such sharing we help prepare the child for the sharing that is an elemental portion of all healthy relationships. Once again, if we can help a child to improve his or her listening skills through the modeling and give and take of conversation at home, we provide them a skill that can take them a long way in future social situations.

E. **Model prosocial skills yourself:** If you ask your child to keep his hands to himself at the dinner table but reach over and slap him for putting his hands in the mashed potatoes what lesson have you taught him? One of the most powerful teaching tools that adults possess is their own behavior. The behavior and actions we model for children have far more impact than our intentions. In fact, regardless of what your wishes, dreams, and intentions are—children will remember what we do and not what we say we do. Therefore, if you wish to help your child develop positive social skills, model them yourself and reinforce them in your child when you see them demonstrated.

F. **Seek ways to teach social skills:** If your child with ADD is in counseling it is important to make sure that some form of attention is being paid to appropriate social skills instruction. At school, if your child is part of a counseling group double check to see how they address the critical area of social skills training. At home, play games that call for appropriate social skills such as following rules, refraining from arguing, taking turns, handling defeat, and cooperation. Sometimes it can be valuable to role-play critical or worrisome situations before they occur. For example, if your son has to give a short presentation in his sixth grade social studies class about the Civil War, have him practice it for you and offer suggestions. If your daughter is worried about how to act at the school dance find out what specifically is worrying her and rehearse how she might handle those situations. If things go wrong for your son or daughter, approach them and ask if you can help.

Then carefully listen to what is troubling them. If they are open to discussion see if you cannot help them to construct alternatives that might have worked better for them and why. In this way you build up the possibility of success in the future—you draw lasting victories from the ashes of present defeats. Find ways to help teach social skills and your child will stand a better chance of both succeeding and learning them.

G. Emphasize process & natural consequences: Rome was not built in a day. Before success will probably come failure. Therefore, if your son or daughter with ADD makes some poor social choices that you are forced to deal with, do so from a consistent and loving perspective and not one tinged with anger & judgment. For example, if your son, whose friends all seem to be ADD, ends up as part of a disciplinary situation at school because of impulsive actions, try to see more than just the need for punishment. Try to help your son to see where his impulsive actions got him and why he strives so hard to fit in even at the expense of his own welfare. Emphasize growth whenever you can. If, for example, through honest effort your son raises his "F" in Spanish to a "D" you can at least point out that his work is now keeping him from failing. Remember, you will teach your child a great deal in terms of how they should act by how you act in critical situations. Make sure that lesson is mature and loving in nature.

H. Understand ADD & its manifestation in your child: You will be unable to adequately address your child's social skills needs if you fail to take the necessary time to learn about his disability and discover his nature. ADD/ADHD takes many forms but there are some commonalities that most parents of children so identified should learn. What message do you send to your child if, despite their having a medical condition, you take no time to learn about that same condition? Likewise, what do we tell a child

15

when our actions all indicate that their interests, needs, problems, and dreams are not even important enough for their own parents to recognize? First strive to understand and then to be understood. In this instance the person and condition you are striving to first understand is your own child & his or her needs. What could be more important?

I. **Teach children to see patterns:** Life is full of patterns and interconnections. Just take a look outside and see how complex and interconnected the entire world is. Likewise, in our own lives, there are patterns that we can discern. For some people, coping with major life changes has always resulted in crisis. For others, whenever they get close to another person they find themselves pushing them away. If we can first recognize such patterns in our lives we can then act to influence them in the future. If we are unaware that such patterns even exist, we may well simply continue them as if our life was running on autopilot. In children's lives adults can first help them to see that patterns are part of many aspects of their daily existence. In math and reading children learn that patterns in numbers & letters mean something. Similarly, if we can help children & adolescents to see that their decisions, actions, and behaviors lead to certain results we set the stage for their becoming more aware of patterns in their own lives. If you can develop a relationship of trust with your child you can share your sense of their own history with them. For example, when your child loses his summer job at Wal-Mart because he got into an argument with his supervisor over something trivial you can help him to make connections to other jobs, friendships, or relationships lost because of his tendency to make mountains out of molehills. If you make this point in a loving rather than judgmental way—maybe he will learn something about himself. Patterns are vital and they can be discovered—but only if we know they even exist.

J. Develop frameworks that kids can understand linked to social skills: There are ways of looking at social behavior that are very insightful. If you can first understand some of these and then teach them to your child, you may well be doing them a great service in terms of their social behavior. Two of these frameworks are the Taoist view of change and the Jahari Window:

Taoist View of Change: Taoism is an ancient Chinese philosophy that emphasizes balance in life. In Taoism even the most wrenching event in a person's life can have value. Indeed, Taoists believe that the greatest difficulties in life may well teach us the most powerful lessons. Or, to put it more simply life's hard blows have three keys:

1. Crisis: The presenting problem that appears insurmountable.

2. Calm: The realization that life will go on despite the loss.

3. Opportunity: The wisdom to see that change holds the seeds of growth.

Similarly, a tool such as **Jahari's Window** allows a youngster to realize that succeeding in the social world requires some insight not only into themselves but also into the world of others. This psychological framework points out that in almost any social encounter there are four key variables in action:

1. What I know about myself.	2. What others know about me

---

3. What I know about myself that others do not know.	4. What others know about me that I do not know.

Through learning that crisis does not mean the end of the world and that taking different perspectives can help you to be more successful, a youngster is better prepared to succeed in life. Adults can help in this learning process by first mastering these skills themselves, taking the time to teach & model them for their children, and then recognizing their use when they occur.

K. **Emphasize appropriate medication management:** If part of your son or daughter's ADD treatment is medication it is essential that you handle this vital component in a thoughtful manner. First, if medication is to be used understand the effects and side effects of the medication of choice. Then be sure that you monitor how your child is handling the medication. Be sure to fill prescriptions and support your child's taking of the medication. Keep track of any relevant behavioral data so that you can contact your child's doctor or psychiatrist if needed. If things are not going well in terms of side effects or key life activities (i.e. school, relationships, etc.) do not hesitate to contact your child's health care professionals. Remember, ADD is a medical diagnosis and, as such, will require careful attention and support from medical staff, counselors, school personnel, and you. If you have decided that medication is a viable option be sure that you take it seriously and monitor your child's well being.

3.

MEDICATION & CHILDREN WITH ADD—
COMMONLY ASKED QUESTIONS

Perhaps the most misunderstood aspect of the treatment of children & adolescents with ADD is the issue of medication. Over the past decade more children in America have started a course of medication therapy due to ADD than any other country in the world. Naturally, this rapid growth in the use of medication for the treatment of ADD has sparked controversy. Some professionals in the medical, educational, or governmental fields point toward this sudden influx of prescriptions as proof of the poor judgment shown by prescribing physicians. In this view, the growth of medication as a primary intervention for ADD is evidence of a conspiracy on the part of drug companies and the medical field to pump up profits at the expense of children. Other critics of the use of various medications with children with ADD point toward the absence of longitudinal studies investigating the effects of medication usage by children. Finally, many professionals and parents fear that the use of medications may promote future drug abuse on the part of youngsters with ADD.

In recent years standards for diagnosing and treating ADD have become more stringent than even five years ago. More and more medical professionals are increasingly conservative in terms of both their willingness to diagnose a youngster with ADD and then to jump to medication as the sole treatment. Still, the field of controlled substances is one that quite naturally raises the eyebrows of parents who confront the decision to have their son or daughter take medication. It is only rational to question the use of any prescription medication with your child. Just because a child has been identified as having ADD does not mean that his or her parents should simply nod their head and then thoughtlessly fill the prescription for Ritalin. No, it is altogether fitting and proper that parents ask hard questions and demand clear & honest answers when it comes to medication.

What follows is a sampling of 20 questions linked to medication usage with children with ADD that we have encountered in our years in the fields of social work and education. In addition, many of these questions are ones we both asked ourselves and the professionals who worked with our own children. Hopefully this Q & A section will offer you some food for thought as you ponder the tough issue of medicating or not medicating your child.

MEDICATION & CHILDREN WITH ADD—20 COMMONLY ASKED QUESTIONS

1. **If my child takes medication will he/she be more prone to drug addiction?** This is a common and understandable fear on the part of many parents. Yet, in reality, the fact that a youngster takes appropriate medication makes it far less likely that they will self-medicate with illegal drugs or alcohol. Children and adolescents who are appropriately medicated make better decisions, act less impulsively, demonstrate improved social skills, are more capable of making positive friendships, and generally make better choices. Medication serves to help youngsters with ADD behave in a more reasonable way.

Therefore, it is far more probable that a youngster with ADD who does not take medication will seek out substances and engage in more risk taking behaviors.

2. **Will my child have to take medication forever?** The length of time a youngster takes medication is based upon their personal growth and development. In some cases a child will remain on some sort of medication regimen into adulthood. In other instances it will only be needed during school years. Each person is a unique individual. The number of years a person needs to remain on ADD medication should be based upon their personal profile and performance. Therefore, that length should vary across people.

3. **Are there alternatives to medications?** Certainly, there are families that have achieved success in treating their children with ADD through the use of approaches such as herbal remedies, a strictly controlled diet, frequent exercise, and behavioral interventions. For example, there are some active children who due to the consumption of specific food colorings or artificial preservatives see their ability to self-regulate their actions decrease. In those circumstances a strictly controlled diet that eliminates the offending additives may have a significant effect upon behavior, concentration, and overall performance. Similarly, research has shown that physical activity releases endorphins and other positive hormones into a person's system. Thus, a child that is regularly active may achieve a more balanced hormonal state and thereby decrease activity levels at other times. However, there is very little research support for these types of interventions and they require an enormous amount of time to carefully monitor the diet or activities of a child. Further, as children move into puberty, natural biochemical changes may cause a careful intervention program to become derailed simply

because the youngster's body chemistry is changing.

4. **What are some common side effects of ADD medications?**
   While side effects vary across medications there are some that may be more common than others. For example, if your child is taking a stimulant medication such as Concerta, Ritalin, or Adderall he or she might experience disruptions to sleep patterns, loss of appetite, concentration problems, moodiness, irritability, drowsiness, or jumpiness. If any of these side effects appear and do not dissipate quickly, or if they are highly disconcerting to your child, you should immediately contact the prescribing physician and attempt a different medication, alter the dosage, or cease medication use altogether. Most children beginning a course of medication will not experience side effects. In some cases the side effects may briefly occur as the child adjusts to the medication. If side effects persist the treatment is not beneficial and should be stopped.

5. **How can I tell if the medication is working?** If you have to ask that question then it probably is not working. Medication should only be used if a child's ADD causes serious loss in terms of behavior. Typically a child taking ADD medication should have demonstrated serious attending, focusing, and other self-control behavior problems prior to the decision to medicate. If the medication is going to have a significant effect it should become apparent within the first few weeks of treatment. Of course, there are varying lengths of time that different medications take to build up to what is called a "therapeutic level" in your child's body. However, after a couple of weeks you should see some change for the better in your child's actions. If not, you should contact the prescribing physician and either adjust the dosage or consider other interventions.

6. **Can medication work alone in treating my child's ADD?** All too many parents, educators, and medical professionals see medication as some sort of "magic bullet" that can cure ADD. This is a falsehood. The best treatment for ADD is a combined approach that includes medication, counseling, behavioral interventions, and a compassionate & loving home. Medication alone will not improve family-school communication or the way you think about your child. No, ADD treatment should be broad-based and all-inclusive.

7. **How do ADD medications work?** Interestingly enough the most commonly used ADD medications are actually stimulants. Drugs such as Dexedrine & Ritalin generally act to speed up a person's metabolism. In people with ADD these same drugs work in what is called a "counter-therapeutic" fashion. That is, instead of speeding a person up they slow them down and allow their mind to work at a speed that is functional. In essence, the medication enhances a child's ability to clearly and patiently process, think, and perceive the world. There have been a number of people with ADD who describe seeing the world "as if the clouds had cleared" after beginning a positive medication regimen.

8. **Should my child stay on the same medication throughout his treatment?** In some cases children remain on a certain medication for quite some time. In other cases changes in medication must occur over a period of years as the effects of what was, at first, an effective medication lessen. This process will vary across individuals but generally some changes will occur over a period of years.

9. **Will my child's dosage ever change?** In all likelihood your child will take differing dosages at different times in his or her life. The simple fact that your child will be growing causes some

adjustment in medication dosage. Further, children entering into adolescence experience significant physical changes. At that time a shift in the effectiveness of certain medications and dosages may play out. Generally speaking, some change in dosage will occur at various times in your child's treatment.

10. **Will insurance cover the cost of my child's medication?** While every policy is slightly to significantly different, by and large insurance will cover at least a share of your child's medication costs. ADD medications are direct treatments for a recognized health condition. ADD is referenced and described in the DSM along with other disorders wherein medication charges are reimbursable. Therefore, if your insurance carrier questions your child's prescription costs be sure to stand your ground and defend his or her right to legitimate medical treatment.

11. **Can the school staff administer my child's medication?** While the law varies from state to state, in general, if your child must have medication at school in order to access learning the district is responsible for making arrangements so that he or she can take medication during the school day. While there may be contractual or legal issues that school officials will have to wrestle with regarding who will either administer or supervise your child's self-administration of medication, in the end the school cannot refuse to handle this issue. This is particularly true if your child has a special education or 504 plan in place that addresses medication in any reasonable way.

12. **Who can prescribe ADD medication?** Medications for the treatment of ADD can only be prescribed by trained medical professionals such as MD's & psychiatrists. Other professionals such as counselors, social workers, and psychologists can make recommendations for medications but the actual prescription must come from a trained physician.

13. How can I have my child assessed? There are many ways to begin an ADD assessment process. Some people simply make an appointment with their child's pediatrician. Other folks seek out a clinic specializing in ADD assessments. In some instances families make use of local mental health centers or university psychology departments to carry out the assessment. What should be borne in mind are two key factors. First, regardless of who makes the diagnosis, only a medical professional can prescribe medication. Second, the more comprehensive the assessment the more honest the diagnosis. While having your doctor simply write a prescription can be a starting point, such a plan is far less comprehensive than having your child go through a comprehensive assessment that is multi-disciplinary in nature. A diagnosis of ADD and resulting treatment is a huge step in your child's life. Should you take that step blindly or with as much information as you can gather?

14. How will the school know about my child's medical needs? School districts can only receive medical information if you give them permission to do so. Therefore, if your child has been identified as having ADD and requiring medication, the only way the district will be informed is if you do so. However, just because you have given the school nurse a copy of the ADD evaluation and prescription does not mean that everyone in the school should know about your child's condition. Only those educators who have an educationally relevant reason to know about your child's condition should do so. Otherwise the school's staff is breaching confidentiality rights that you and your child possess.

15. Should I get some sort of school reports to help my doctor? Yes, all too often the child's physician, counselor, and school staff never exchange information. In this way they all work in good faith but with one hand tied behind their back. You should request periodic teacher reports which you, in turn, can share with your child's doctor and counselor. In this way everyone is working to meet the best interests of the child. Think of your child as at the center of a wagon wheel. Each of the spokes leading back to the wheel's center represents some form of support given to your child. In turn the spokes can be seen as your child's teacher, counselor, school principal, doctor, psychiatrist, parents, siblings, and friends. The child remains at the center with the spokes coming together there.

16. **Should my child take medication on the weekends, during school holidays, and in the summer?** This is a question that may have varying answers. For example, if your child experiences some side effects but has shown marked improvement at school, you may wish to consider giving him or her breaks from medication when school is not in session. On the other hand, some children are so disruptive when they are off their medication that it may be destructive to them and others to have them yo-yoing on and off of medication. It is not uncommon for children to stop taking their medications during prolonged school breaks such as at holidays or during the summer. This is a prime question to discuss with your child's treatment team and your child him or herself.

17. **What are the long-term effects of ADD medications on children?** There really is no long-term research available in this area. That statement is one of the primary reasons why some families choose to decline the option of having their children take medication. However, there is a great deal of research that points toward the problems that "at risk" students experience both in school and in adulthood. Children who struggle in school with issues linked to academic performance, behavior, attendance, and decision making are far more likely to drop out of school, under

achieve, or run into community-based problems. Frequently, referrals to special education for behavioral and emotional concerns are linked to youngsters who demonstrate symptoms of undiagnosed ADD or who were once identified as having ADD but went untreated. Yes, you should be very cautious about taking the "medication step." Of course, you should carefully monitor your child's behavior, any medication side effects, and overall performance. Certainly, you should listen to how your child describes his or her feelings about taking medication & how the treatment feels. However, it is unwise to think that problems your child is experiencing that are linked to a medical condition will simply go away over time without treatment.

18. **Can ADD occur along with ailments?** Very often youngsters with ADD will also show symptoms that can be linked to ailments such as depression or anxiety. In fact, in a number of instances physicians treating a youngster for ADD are actually dealing with depression or anxiety. The concept of "co-morbidity" is one that exists in the ADD world. Co-morbidity refers to the presentation of symptoms for separate ailments that overlap. For example, a child who is depressed may demonstrate poor concentration, sleep disorders, loss of appetite, withdrawal from social situations, and emotionality. Similarly, any or all of those symptoms can also be manifested in incidences of ADD. Therefore, it is even more important to make sure that your child's initial assessment is comprehensive and considers not just ADD but also any other potential illnesses. The treatment of depression, anxiety, and ADD are similar but distinctly different. For example, medications commonly used to treat ADD can worsen depression or anxiety. Make sure your child is properly assessed and diagnosed so that this sort of problem does not make your child's life worse.

19. **How seriously should I take my child when he tells me he hates the way his medication makes him feel?** It is never wrong to carefully listen to your child when he or she is sharing something important with you. If your child tells you that he or she hates or is troubled by how the medication makes them feel, take those words seriously. Report what your child is telling you to the treating physician as soon as possible. Make sure the medical professionals are listening to you and what your child is saying. A change in prescription, dosage, or treatment may well be in order. Remember, ADD is a long-term condition. If your child's treatment is making him or her suffer, it must be changed in order to assure some reasonable hope of future improvement.

20. **If I refuse to have my child take medication can the school district ignore his or her ADD diagnosis?** No, even if you refuse to use medication to treat your child's ADD his or her condition still exists. However, if your child truly needs medication to function there may be little that school-based interventions can achieve. A child with an ADD diagnosis may be found eligible for support services under Section 504 or special education regardless of the use or non-use of medication. However, the school district may be forced to treat your child's learning and behavioral symptoms as if they were a learning disability or emotional disorder if you do not appropriately treat your child.

In the end, this series of twenty questions is far from comprehensive in nature. However, in looking back at the broad issue of medication and children with ADD some key points emerge:

a. Each child is unique and so too should their treatment be.

b. There are non-medication interventions for children with ADD.

c. Prevailing research would point toward the need for a multi-faceted treatment plan for ADD that includes counseling, medication, and other supports.

d. Negative side effects can occur when ADD medication is used.

e. Close communication between home, school, and medical staff is important.

f. Medication dosages and prescriptions may change over the course of a child's treatment.

g. It is important to observe and listen to children at home in order to see how their treatment is working.

h. ADD can be co-morbid with other ailments like depression & anxiety.

i. Medication is not a "magic bullet" that will wipe away all the problems that make up your child's ADD.

4.

Understanding the Conflict Cycle: Survival Skills for Parenting Your Child with ADD

You come home after a long, hard day at work. Immediately your son who has ADD begins to demand your attention. Before you can even get your coat off he's after you, "Can we go to Blockbuster, I want to rent a video game? Can we go now—is it OK?" You stop and think for a second and remember that your son has lost video game privileges because of poor grades in school. When you remind him of this fact he responds by saying, "That's not fair! Do you really think taking my games away is going to make me like school? That sucks!" You can feel the irritation start to rise up in you. Just yesterday, you sat down with your son and worked out a fair consequence for his low grades. At that time he seemed to understand the equity of losing his video game privileges—but today, it's a different story. Every effort you make to remind him of the connection between earned rewards and good work is met by, "Whatever!" or "That's not fair—can we still go to Blockbuster?" In the end you and your son get into a whopper of a fight that results in your blood pressure soaring and your son slamming his way into his room with this parting shot, "All you care about is school—you just don't get it—I hate you!"

If this scenario sounds at all familiar you have lived what most parents of children with ADD experience on a regular basis. Youngsters with ADD can be extremely bright, but, they are impulsive and often act without thinking. At one moment they are nodding in understanding of what their parents or teachers are saying to them. The next moment, they are doing exactly the opposite of what they agreed was reasonable. How can a rational adult deal with these flights of impulsivity and bad judgment?

Conflict is a part of life but it can also be a pathway to death. While most people will experience some levels of conflict or stress in their daily lives, too much of it can result in serious, and even debilitating illness. In a family situation the greater the conflict the less time there is available for love and acceptance. If the members of a family are always at one another's throats because of problems, how can they come together in a supportive manner? Handling conflict, its preliminary clues, and the aftereffects of fighting are all essential survival skills for anyone attempting to raise a child or adolescent with ADD.

What follows are twelve suggestions centered in on the broad area of managing conflict. Each of these suggestions comes from both practical experience and ideas drawn from relevant readings. While no single one of these alternatives is a "magic bullet" for handling the tough situations that come up with kids, they can provide reasonable food for thought. Hopefully these ideas can spawn even better ones that are relevant to your own family and, in that way, help you to address the potentially exhausting and harmful ritual of daily conflict.

I. **What is the real issue?** When you end up fighting with your son because of the fact that he spends too much time playing video games is the real issue the games or something else? In many arguments, once the dust has settled, the events that triggered the fight seem trivial. In most cases there is an underlying issue that causes the fight to occur. While your son's persistence in playing hours of video games may trigger the fight, the real causes could be his lack of attention to homework, the fact that he spends little time with you & other family members, or the fact that you simply do not understand why video games are any fun. If you can identify what the "big picture" issue is you may avoid getting caught up in arguments over "small potatoes" concerns. For example, if the real issue linked to your son's video game habit is the fact that he is failing two classes, link his being able to play games to having satisfactorily completed his homework. Make sure he shows you the work and go over it with him. In this way you are spending time together, he is led to understand that life offers natural consequences, and you are fair. If you end up fighting because you just don't get the value of video games, ask if you can watch him play some of his games. That time together, while your son carries out one of his favorite activities, may build understanding and patience.

II. **Are you personalizing things too much?** When your child says, "I hate you!" it certainly can hurt. However, in moat cases, those words are uttered in the height of anger and should not be taken too seriously. When people are upset they say and do things they will later regret. If we personalize a child's anger we play right into the conflict cycle. We take the harsh words into our soul and give them far more power than they would otherwise have. Likewise, when we personally attack a child we cross a line that borders just parental discipline with emotional abuse. It is one thing to greet a child's poor report card with, "I am very disappointed with you Greg. These grades are far lower than you led me to believe they would be. I feel you have betrayed us and, more importantly, yourself." It is a far different story to say, "My God how did this happen? This is the worst report card I have ever seen. You really have been a loser this past quarter. You know, that one teacher is right—you are lazy!" When we take in other people's anger as part of our personality we wound ourselves in an unnecessary way. When we call a child names we wound them, damage their trust in us, and build up a wellspring of poor self-imagery in a youngster who may really be doing everything they possibly can but is still failing.

III. **Are you focusing on the issue at hand?** Your daughter impulsively grabs the television's remote control from your younger son and changes the channel without asking permission. A fight ensues that features wailing, yelling, and name-calling. You intervene and say, "Jane, you always behave this way. Why can't we ever have a moment's peace? I don't think you are ever going to get it! Go to your room—you're grounded forever." Although it is easier said than done, it is important to focus on the issue at hand without becoming too grandiose. In fights between marital partners words such as "always," "never," and "forever" are ones that carry a tremendously negative energy charge. How would you react if a person said to you, "You are never going to amount to anything!" That person probably would not stay on your Christmas card list. Therefore, why would we take an irritating problem and label a child we love as hopeless. When we get carried away in our criticism we make our ability to solve a problem much less than it can be. Focus on the issue at hand, avoid over arching labels, and try to stay in control."

IV. **Have you taken a deep breath?** Children with ADD can drive you crazy. Their relentless energy, driving need for attention, and impulsive actions are a surefire pathway to exhaustion. But, they are your children and their needs did not come out of thin air. When you start to feel anger well up inside of yourself because your son or daughter refuses to take no for an answer or is otherwise accelerating a conflict situation, take a deep breath. If you need to—remove yourself from the situation and tell your child you are not going to discuss this until you have calmed down and so have they. Pause and say to yourself or out loud, "Wow, I'm really angry—I need to take a break from this." It is better to take a deep breath and then get back to the problem than to let your anger accelerate and only make things worse. When you are breathing try not to think about the situation at hand. In fact—just breathe and count your breaths. After ten breaths check and see if you feel able to continue the discussion. If not—breathe some more and get back together with your child when you are ready. This action is better than just throwing the gasoline of more and more anger on the fire of your fight with your child.

V. **Have you tried the "tag-team" approach?** In police work there is the old interrogation approach that pairs a "good cop" with a "bad cop." In professional wrestling, some of the most entertaining events are those that feature tag-team pairings. In raising children, if you and your partner can develop a tag-team approach to solving problems you will be far ahead of the game. For whatever reasons, some situations anger some people more than others. If the argument you are having with your child is causing you to become more and more angry, do not be too proud to tag off and let your partner handle things for a while. There is no gain to be found in simply battering away at one another if an impasse has been reached. It is far better to turn things over to your mate and let him or her try to achieve a better result. Effective tag-teams share similar fundamental values so one partner is not always the good or bad cop. However, if you are pounding your head against a wall, let your partner try a different approach. For example, if you struggle to get your son out of bed in the morning and it generally results in an angry start to the day, switch chores with your partner, and let him or her take over that part of the morning routine.

VI. **Are you imposing your reality on the situation?** You and your child are two linked but still separate & unique people. Just because you liked or disliked certain things in your own world does not mean your child will follow suit. For example, if you are an ADD father and your son has ADD, it does not mean that he will enjoy exactly the same things you do. You may have found sports to be a wonderful outlet for you to use your high energy and recklessness in a productive manner. ON the other hand, your son may choose to become artistic and enjoy fantasy books, movies, and video games. Do not impose your reality on your children. If you do you misstep in two critical ways. First, you fail to recognize and bond with the person your child really is. Second, you will fail in your efforts to falsely mold your child in your own image and in trying to do this act you will build barriers between each other.

VII. Are you disengaging when appropriate or accelerating conflict?

In many arguments there is a time when only diminishing returns can occur if it continues. Have you ever argued with someone and then said something that you always regretted saying? There is no shame, and potentially great gain, in disengaging from a damaging fight. When you see your child or yourself at the boiling point notice it and say, "I think we need some space. Let's talk about this later." The longer you stay in an accelerating battle the more casualties will occur. Also, once a situation has started to calm down do you ever dredge up the old issue or new ones, only to start up the fight again? Once peace has begun to reappear never throw it away so you can get the last word in or feel temporarily justified because you defended your pride. Once you stir things up again it can only get worse. Know when to back off and give yourself and your family a chance for peace.

VIII. Do you know you family members and your own hot buttons? Many people have certain hot buttons that, if pushed,

will cause them to become upset. For example, you may hate the idea of being compared to your mother because she represented a weak person who never really understood you. Then, in the middle of a disagreement with your partner, he or she says, "You know, you're acting just like your mother. I should have realized when I married you that I was really marrying your mom!" Well, that probably is not a way of alleviating anger and tension in that situation. Likewise, over time, if we are paying attention we should know what the hot buttons are for our family members. If, in the heat of battle, we choose to push those buttons we can only blame ourselves for the reactions we receive. Avoid those hot buttons and work to lessen the impact that pushing your own ones generates. The longer we allow past wrongs to control present behavior the greater power we give to them. Know what trips your trigger and work on it. Know where your family member's triggers are and refrain from pulling them.

IX. **Do you make mountains out of molehills?** Your son comes home fifteen minutes past his curfew and you jump on him, "Where have you been. We really can't trust you at all. March right up to your room. You're grounded and that's the last time in years that you'll be driving my car anywhere!" In this situation you have not even given the boy a chance to explain why he was marginally late. Immediately, you have jumped all over your son and punished him to the hilt without really understanding what even happened. When we take small situations and build them up into monumental ones we act in an utterly self-defeating manner. If being fifteen minutes late results in this sort of reaction, how probable is it that if your son has a really serious problem he will dare to come and talk to you about it? Children and adolescents with ADD are guilty of some really foolish and destructive behavior. In those sorts of situations a responsible parent must take their child's actions seriously. But much of life is not that serious. Know what is a major issue and what is not and act accordingly.

X. Are you sucked into the battle? There are people who just like to argue. Some of those folks are children or adolescents and some of them are adults. If you find yourself frequently battling your children stop and think about this question, "Who owns the problem?" If you reflect on this simple question and discover that by getting sucked into fight after fight, you are actually making things worse—then stop! Your life, and the lives of your children, will be fairly unfulfilling if you are always fighting with one another. Is there something you are doing that makes the fights both more frequent and worse than they need to be? Take stock of your contributions to the daily battles. Be honest with yourself and ask yourself, "Am I doing things that make things worse?" Try to ask your children what their perspectives are. Perhaps, in asking you can discover what it is that you do which sets them off. In a nutshell, do not get sucked into an endless cycle of conflict. Down that pathway lies a life akin to what Israelis and Palestinians have lived for decades—endless war with no peace on the horizon.

XI. Can you see your child's fear & insecurity beneath the surface of their anger? You are arguing with your son about his grades when he shouts, "I don't care about school—whatever." You immediately launch into a long rant about how without an education he will be nothing but a bum when he sullenly walks away from you. All too often people wallpaper their true feeling over with a covering of indifference in order to mask what they really feel. A child with ADD who is struggling in school knows how embarrassing that can be. Perhaps he has taken an "I don't care" attitude in order to protect himself from the pain that facing his problems might cause. Maybe, he really does try hard but still fails. Often, just beneath the surface of the irritating or seemingly unmotivated exterior, lies a heart that is in pain. If we respond to a person's pain by punishing them, berating them, or calling them lazy we ally ourselves with all the other people in the child's world who have already made him feel terrible. Of course, a responsible parent must strive to help their son or daughter do the best they can. But, are we a friend to a child if, at their low point when they are already in a hole, we shovel dirt in on top of their head? Even though it can be terribly frustrating when our children do poorly and seem indifferent, they remain our children. By being patient, seeking them out, asking them what's wrong, securing help, and staying both responsible and loyal we offer them far more hope than when we simply criticize them.

XII. Do you have a united parental front? It is hard enough to raise a child without him or her having a disability like ADD. It can be even more challenging to rear children who, due to their ADD, struggle with school, friendships, work skills, or other elements of daily living. This task can become almost impossible if both parents are not on the same page about their child's needs. Imagine a scenario where one parent of a child with ADD sees him as lazy while the other one sees him as misunderstood and always worthy of enabling support. That circumstance is a surefire way to end up in even more familial conflict than you could imagine. If you wish to be successful in raising your child with ADD you must have a reasonable and united parental front. If one of you is always giving in to the demands of your child while the other is unbending in his or her discipline, you will end up fighting not only with your child but with your partner as well. It is important that you and your partner have a general agreement about key issues like medication, counseling, schoolwork, school-family communication, and home-based consequences. If you punish your child only to find out that you partner has rewarded him or her for the same actions you will soon find yourself at odds with everyone in your family. A united front shows your child that you and your partner respect one another and love him or her enough to act together in support of them.

5.

Homework is Hell!

You have tried and tried to understand your son or daughter with ADHD. But, every time you sit down to do homework—your life becomes hell. Stop and think for a few seconds about the many fights, battles, tears, and raised voices you can remember that really revolved around one terrible issue—HOMEWORK! Then ask yourself, "Do you want to be your child's teacher?" If not, then here are some tips for you when dealing with what may be one of the biggest bugaboos about school and kids with ADHD. Each suggestion follows some commonly held false beliefs about homework completion and all that goes along with that difficult task.

Ten Ways to go Crazy or Stay Sane
When Trying to get Homework Done:

Fallacy #1:   Always make your child do his or her homework immediately after school. Just think; school is hard enough for your child to cope with. Maybe the past few hours of the school day have been spent staring at the clock—wishing for the day to end. Now you meet your son or daughter at the door and greet them with the terrible words, "Get your homework out—you can't do anything until you've got it all done!" Wow—that certainly is a good way to get your quality time with your child off to a good start!

Suggestion: Allow your child to have some "decompression" time after school to relax and get the kinks out of the day before plunging into the homework. Set up a schedule that fits your family and child's needs. Then use that schedule to work on homework. Perhaps getting things done right away works for you and your child? However, think about it, if getting through a school day for a child with ADHD is like running a marathon—does it not make sense to give him or her a breather before you lunge into a ten-K run?

Fallacy #2: Always complete every single bit of the work no matter how long it takes. In our work with children and families it has been our common experience to hear parents say things like, "Oh yes, we spend at least three or four hours trying to get all the homework done." While many of those folks have good intentions—the result is disastrous. Try to imagine how much stress, pain, and anguish is created when people who love one another spend that much time fighting about a task that really is undoable.

Suggestion: Set a reasonable time limit to the amount of work your family and your child with ADHD can cope with. No family will prosper if they are spending four hours nightly in battles over the completion of math assignments and book reports. If your child has a 504 plan or IEP make sure language is included that addresses reasonable homework accommodations inclusive of setting daily time limits. Although things vary from place to place and child to child, the following homework time limits may be worth considering:

Grades K-3 no more than 30-45 minutes per day
Grades 3-5 no more that 45 –60 minutes per day
Grades 6-8 no more than 60-75 minutes per day
Grades 9-12 no more than 90 minutes per day

Fallacy #3:   Always believe that all homework has value. If you buy this line of thinking then every single math problem, worksheet, grammar assignment, and word search that comes home as homework is as important as finding the actual key to world peace. In reality homework should only be information that a child can do independently. In fact, in numerous educational reports homework is described as legitimate if the child can understand at least 95% of it without adult support. If a child cannot grasp homework then the actual instruction in class has failed. Also, homework should not be "busy work." If your son or daughter is bringing home a number of game activities, word searches, crossword puzzles, or canned worksheets it may be symptomatic of such "busy work."

Suggestion: If you think that your son or daughter has too much homework schedule a meeting with the teacher and discuss modifications. If you meet with cooperation—great! If, on the other hand, you meet with resistance—look into the processes that need to be completed to complete a 504 or special education evaluation of your child. It is within your right to make such a request and what is more important your child's welfare or the feelings of school staff who do not seem to get it.

Fallacy #4:   By forcing my son or daughter to be responsible about getting all the homework done I will help him or her to develop improved organizational and work skills. Think about that belief statement the next time you are fighting with your child who says they hate you with tear filled eyes. All that pain and conflict in a family create are barriers to happiness. Why make completing every bit of the homework another pathway to discord in your family?

Suggestion: Find things that your son or daughter is good at or which they like to do and make those the focal point of your efforts to encourage an improved work ethic. If your son loves to hike in the woods—take him on backpacking trips. There is no better place to demonstrate a good work ethic while also learning a great deal about both himself and your relationship with him than in the woods. If your daughter likes to draw, frame some of her work and encourage her talent. Every child has gifts. Use those gifts as the way to encourage productivity while cementing your loving relationship together. Do not play to people's weaknesses and expect things to work out well.

Fallacy #5: Believe the lie that only you should be responsible for getting your child's homework done. All too many parents feel a great weight upon their shoulders because of the difficulties that raising a child with ADHD can create. Homework can be one of the cement blocks you carry around on your back in this regard. Do not pick up that painful burden if you can find a good alternative.

Suggestion: If you can afford it, hire a tutor to help work with your child for a few hours per week. If not, ask older siblings to help your child with ADHD on projects & studies. Involve your son or daughter in after school study groups. Check with the school about peer or staff tutoring options. Consult with your church about study groups. Look into service organizations to see if there are any means to offer help in terms of getting homework done. In a nutshell—farm out the work as much as you can. If homework is creating a barrier between you and your child, and you love your child, then find alternatives that spread out the work and better that precious relationship.

Fallacy #6: If we repeat this work enough times my child will remember it. Time and again we have heard parents of children with ADHD say that they work and work with their child hoping that the information will finally stick. When we hear these words it is often easy to almost see these well-intended folks banging their heads against a concrete wall.

Suggestion: ADHD can affect memory. In some cases no matter how hard you try there will be a "spaciness" that colors your child's ability to recall information on demand. When you add tension or stress to the equation—things only get worse. If after a few trials your son or daughter is not getting some point of learning—stop, move on to something else, take a break, stretch, laugh about it, and lessen the tension. Do not keep hammering away until both you and your child are at a point of total frustration. Think about it, how would you feel if another adult keep pushing and pushing at you to do something you did not understand? Would that situation sit well with you or would you get frustrated? Frustration blocks learning—know when to back off and things will go more smoothly.

Fallacy #7:   Even though your child struggles with writing and has terrible handwriting skills you push and push to have him or her complete every paper and pencil task as assigned. In doing this you believe that with some extra practice your child's handwriting and written language skills will get better

Suggestion: Difficulties in penmanship and writing kills are among the most frequently noted problems that children and adolescents with ADHD demonstrate. Therefore, get with the program and find alternative ways to help your child complete written assignments. If you have a computer at home remember, "It's never too soon to introduce word processing!" In the elementary grades have your child dictate work to you while you word process it. At the intermediate grades help your child to either independently or with your assistance complete assignments on the computer. Be sure your child knows how to use spell and grammar checks so the middle school book reports are readable. At the high school level be sure that all written work is completed on a computer so that your son or daughter is not penalized due to their sloppy handwriting. There is no law that says a child's Math, Literature, English, or History assignments must be scrawled in their own writing rather than typed. If you do not have a computer you can still copy out the answers your child dictates to you. Be sure the teacher or teachers are aware of your practices and the reason why dictation is necessary. Remember, the world your child will grow up into will feature more, not less, computer usage. Therefore, why not use technology as a tool just as your child will have to do when he or she grows up. Also, do not be concerned about using proper typing skills. People can "hunt and peck" very fast on a computer keyboard.

Fallacy #8:   You believe that once you start working it is important to plow on through all the work before any fun things can happen. In this school of thought you hold on to the concept that if you take a break or switch gears away from homework, your child will never get started again and the world will end.

Suggestion: Most union contracts have language that deals with lunch times, breaks, holidays, and length of the workday. The reason collective bargaining agreements have language like this is because people are not robots. Yes, having a reasonable schedule to complete your child's homework is a good thing. However, people are unique and times change. Just because your schedule says that from 6:30-8:00 is homework time does not mean that it must be a solid ninety minutes of non-stop homework fun. No, gauge each day based upon how you and your child are feeling as well as the changing work expectations that arise. If it is final exam week at the high school you probably will be spending some concentrated time studying with your child. On the other hand, if your elementary-aged son is squirming even more than usual while you study spelling words—perhaps a break is in order. Allowing for breaks before plunging into concentrated academics is a common accommodation in children with ADHD's special education and 504 plans. Why not follow suit at home? Think about it, if you had to report to work and labor non-stop throughout the whole day without taking any sort of break your productivity would eventually dip. Keep that thought in mind and allow for breaks so that your own child can catch his or her breath before returning to the homework wars.

Fallacy #9: Hold on to the false hope that your child with ADHD will become consistent despite their disability. Even though your son or daughter remembers things on one day but not the next you hold dear to your heart the belief that if he or she only tried harder they could always remember things. In fact, if your child just was not so "lazy" they could do so much better.

Suggestion: Kids with ADHD are maddeningly inconsistent. For example, an evening can be spent drilling spelling words into your child's head only to keep hearing the same mistakes time after time. Yet, the next morning that same child can tell you with 90% accuracy how to spell the words correctly. You leave such encounters pulling your hair out and wondering, "Why is this happening?" The reality is that ADHD is a condition that breeds inconsistency and impulsivity. Expect these two characteristics and do not punish your child or yourself by trying to will them away. The word "lazy" is one of the most powerful words in our language. When we call someone "lazy" we indict him or her in so many ways. Time and again we have heard teachers and parents label children "lazy" even though that same child is trying so hard to please them. Would you call a child who was blind "clumsy" because they bumped into furniture in unfamiliar rooms? Of course not, because that child's disability is obvious. But, sometimes we leap to judgment and label kids with ADHD "lazy" because they do not get everything done in the way we want them to. By labeling such a child as "lazy" we lessen them and demonstrate our own misunderstanding of both their disability and their spirit. Expect and work with inconsistency or destroy your relationship with the child.

Fallacy #10:   No matter what anyone else says I know my child best. Even though the school tells me that my son is misbehaving in school I know that he's right and everyone is against him. If my daughter comes home with a complaint about her teacher I will always take her word at face value. The school staff is always to be distrusted and cannot tell me anything about my child. I will always fight for my children even if doing so hurts them.

Suggestion: Sometimes when we listen to others rather than immediately becoming defensive we can be our children's best allies. There are some terrible people who work in school systems but they are not the norm. Work very hard to establish a partnership with the school staff in order to make things better, not worse, for your child. If you can develop and maintain good communication with your child's teachers only good things can result. Be sure to inform your child's teachers of his or her condition and educational & social needs. Prepare a one-page fact sheet about your child and his or her condition. Make sure your child's teachers are aware and knowledgeable about his or her condition, academic needs, accommodation plan, unique skills, and your communication expectations. Come to school meetings prepared but willing to listen and not just demand or criticize. The word partnership infers equal sharing of emotion, information, compassion, and love. By establishing a partnership you assist your child without enabling them. Kids do stupid things. Your own children are not immune to this reality. Therefore, if something goes wrong at school do not always assume that your child or the school staff is always right or wrong. If you always belittle school staff members at home in front of your child how much respect do you think he or she will feel toward them at school? Remember, eventually your son or daughter will have to function as an adult without you there to run interference for them. Be sure they learn the academic and social skills they need to be successful and independent despite their disability.

CONCLUSION

Homework can be hell but it is a predictable one. If you ignore your child's condition and try to plow through work that they struggle with you will fail. If you ignore your child's disability and make no accommodations for it at home or at school only bad things can happen. For kids with ADHD schoolwork can be a real cross to bear. Do you want to help them bear it or hold a whip in hand as they plod on? Hopefully by recognizing your son or daughter's needs, applying reasonable expectations, showing compassion, and making sure you establish a meaningful partnership with the school staff you can be a very loving factor in this potentially frustrating part of growing up. The alternative is to make things worse and damage both your child and yourself.

6.

Selecting a Counselor:
The Leap Into the Great Unknown

Many times parents of a child with ADHD will meet with school personnel only to be asked, "Have you ever thought about counseling for Johnny?" In all too many of those situations the family has thought about counseling but has no idea how to arrange it. As a result, one of the best potential pathways to help is left untraveled.

Selecting a counselor for your child is no easy matter. There are many people out there who say they are experts in counseling kids with ADHD but many of them are not. When accepting the need for counseling a parent may struggle to figure out how exactly to find the right person for their child. A quick glimpse at the yellow pages under the heading of "counselor" may well reveal a number of possibilities—but how do you find a good person?

While there are a number of ways to get a referral to a counselor a few may have more value than others. If you think your son or daughter will benefit from counseling you could ask any or all of the following sources for a reasonable referral:

- School Counselors
- School social workers
- Friends who have had children counseled for similar concerns

- The local Mental Health Center
- Your Local Hospital
- Your Family Physician
- Internet-Based Family Support Groups Specializing in ADHD
- Your clergyman or woman

None of these sources is foolproof and all of them depend upon your level of trust for the person or people filling those roles. However, finding a person who might counsel your child is just the first step. Next you have to discover if that professional counselor is well matched to not only your child but also your entire family.

Once you have decided to contact a counselor you should begin a "shopping process." Remember, regardless of how well recommended this counselor may be, he or she may not be right for your family. When you first speak with the potential counselor be prepared to interview them just as they are interviewing you and your child as possible clients. Keep in mind that you are the consumer and the potential counselor must fit your niche in the counseling marketplace. You would not buy a car without test-driving it would you? Therefore, do not be shy in asking specific questions about issues that are relevant to your child's ADHD. Among such question areas could be some of the following:

- How well does the counselor understand and consult with schools? Remember, your child's ADHD does not exist only at home. If the counselor is a novice about schools he or she will be of limited assistance with many of the issues & problems your child and you face in regards to school performance.

- Is the counselor skilled in both individual and family-based approaches? Some counselors are excellent at working with individual children but remain isolated from the broader family situation. Generally, such an isolated approach will have far more limited results than one that includes working with other family members as well.

- How well does the potential counselor understand that there are many facets to the world of a child with ADHD? For example, when describing his or her potential course of treatment does the counselor speak about not only the child with ADHD but also factors such as is ADHD a family trait, how well are siblings coping with the ADHD issues, is one parent more frustrated than another, what is happening at school.

- How well does the counselor begin to identify any key areas of frustration that you and your child face? A counselor who begins to describe or ask about issues that are of great concern to you in your first contact with them is one to strongly consider hiring. If, on the other hand, the potential counselor never reflects back any of your concerns or neglects to ask questions about matters you see as key—beware.

- Is the counselor open to family-based strengths or does he or she seem like they cannot wait to "fix your family?" There are some counselors who believe their job is to strip away everything that is "wrong" in a person's life and then help rebuild things. This is a dangerous approach and one that is based more on the therapist's ego than an actual desire to help others. Be careful if you see the counselor as overly critical at the outset.

- How well trained is the counselor in the area of ADHD? What types of training has he or she recently completed? There are a lot of folks who purport to know how to treat children and adults with ADHD. Some of them are very expert. Others are not.

If the counselor does not impress you with their understanding of ADHD—look elsewhere.

- What psychiatric or medical doctor backup does the counselor have? Who do they consult with and refer to for medication management? While medication is not always part of a child with ADHD's treatment, it often is. If your counselor is not connected to an MD or psychiatrist who can monitor medication needs your child's treatment will become more complicated and disjointed.

- Will the counselor accept crisis calls? Not all counselors are willing to handle crisis. If your child and family see crisis management as a potential or actual need then you must find a counselor who will take your phone calls when the crisis arrives.

- How familiar is the counselor with ADHD rating scales and assessments? Counseling cannot be conducted in a bubble. In many, if not most, cases a child with ADHD will experience some school problems. These problems can be minor or very traumatic. Unless the potential counselor is familiar with the types of assessments that are typically used to measure the effects of ADHD at school, how can he or she possibly get a clear picture of your child's life?

- Will the counselor set a clear time line and workable therapy goals? This process may take some time but early on in treatment it is recommended that the counselor share with you a potential time line for treatment as well as realistic goals for the process. The time line may be somewhat vague but should at least begin to state how long he or she thinks it will be necessary for your child to be in counseling. Goals should be developed in conjunction with input from your child and the entire family. They should be realistic and not impossible to achieve. For example, if your child's counselor recommends the following goal you should at the very least question him or her about it, "In the next three months Greg will demonstrate the ability to follow all parental and teacher directions." This type of goal is vague, unrealistic, and difficult to measure. It is also very unlikely to be achieved.

- Will the counselor periodically meet with you and other family members to update progress and get feedback? While the main client is the child with ADHD, your child does not live in a vacuum. Periodic visits with you and your family can help keep therapy "real."

- Does the counselor have a sense of humor? Life is too important to be taken seriously all the time. A counselor has to deal with gut-wrenching issues. However, life can be so complex that we have to have a sense of humor to sometimes endure it. A humorless counselor is one to avoid.

- Why does the counselor feel he or she is qualified to treat your child & why do they feel that way? This question is critical and it is just like the type of question a potential new boss asks you when he or she says, "Why are you the right person for the job?" If you are not comfortable with the counselor's answer—do not buy their services.

Once you have made a selection of a counselor for your child it is important that you keep your expectations for counseling results realistic. Remember, it took a lot of years for you and your child to reach the new counselor's doorstep. Change can happen but it probably will not occur overnight. Remain connected to your child's therapy but also remember:

- Things may get worse before they get better. Just the act of beginning to recognize the problems that exist can often result in some unhappy feelings. In counseling sometimes a person has to first begin to feel sadness, loss, or pain before they can deal with them. If things do not get better right away after counseling begins—be patient.

- Do not pry into your child's counseling sessions. A good counselor will involve you and your family in the counseling process to the extent that confidentiality permits. If you are constantly prodding your child and the counselor for information about the sessions you will build a barrier between yourself and your child's treatment. Stay connected but allow your child enough space to be honest in his or her counseling sessions.

- Do not expect a miracle cure. In counseling trained professionals work to help clients displace more poorly constructed parts of their lives with more functional ones. The counselor does not work to replace behaviors, emotions, or ideas. No, he or she works with the client to search out how he or she feels, how those feelings influence behavior, any patterns of behavior, and better ways to cope with life. This takes time and effort—it will not happen in the blink of an eye.

- Accept paradoxical ideas. If counseling is going well you may find your child saying or doing less outrageous things. However, ADHD by its very nature leads to impulse and misunderstanding. Effective counselors may respond to such regressive thinking in a paradoxical manner. For example, a teenage boy comes into his therapy session and says, "I'm dropping out of school and there's nothing anyone can do about it!" The counselor may respond by saying, "Well, that's an idea—it may not be in your best interests but, why not, what have you got to lose?" Then, over the remainder of the session the counselor may well work to help the teen understand what he has to lose by a decision that has lifelong costs associated with it. You do not have to meet every battle head on. By responding in an unpredictable way that avoids immediate conflict you may do better with your child. Therefore, if your child's counselor talks to you about paradoxical responses do not immediately reject them as catering to your crazy kid.

- Remember—the first few sessions are really not counseling; they are trust building. Counseling has no chance of success if trust is not established between the client and the counselor. A good counselor will take the first series of sessions to establish some trust and understanding with their client. It is only after that rapport has been established that goals and time lines can be created. It is also only after that relationship development that good work can begin in the sessions.

- If your child comes home and talks about occasionally playing games in therapy ask about them but do not reject them as a waste of time. Sometimes the best way to establish trust and break through defenses is to have a child play a game they are interested in or comfortable with. For example, a child who is busy playing a computer games they like may well be more willing to share information with a counselor because their guards are down. Counseling needs to be far more than just playing games but do not get worried if your child sometimes talks about them, as part of his or her sessions.

- Just because a child resists therapy does not mean it is not working. If your son or daughter bitterly fights you to go to counseling you need to find out why. However, if your child grumbles but goes, count your blessings. It can be very difficult to get to the heart of your own problems, emotions, deficits, and defeats. Sometimes a client may well not feel like that battle is one they always want to fight. However, counseling that is working will lead to tough issues. Hang in there and help your sometimes reluctant child to do so as well. Praise your child for the work they are doing in counseling and be a support of that good work rather than a barrier.

- Cooperate with the counselor when he or she asks for information. It is important for a counselor to have a sense of the environment within which their client is functioning. So, if your child's counselor asks you for teacher reports, some family background information, or health updates provide them. If you want to know why the counselor needs that information— ask. If the answer seems reasonable—cooperate. If you feel uncomfortable with the request—tell the counselor and work it out.

- Stay in close contact with your child's counselor. Make sure you show appropriate interest in the counseling process without violating your child's emotional space. Make sure your child knows how much you love and support him or her. By finding the right counselor, supporting that process, being a part of it to the extent that works, and being open to new suggestions or behaviors you serve your child well. Counseling can be one of the most vital elements of your child's treatment plan. Be sure you help make the counseling process a strong pillar of support for your child and not just another disappointment.

7.

ADHD CHECKMATE:

RULES FOR THE GAME OF LIFE

Living or working with a person with ADHD can be a very frustrating experience. The shopping list that was so carefully made out can be overwhelmed by impulse buying. Conversations started in good faith swiftly lose steam, as concentration is lost. Working on in-class or homework assignments becomes as much fun as having a root canal. Stop for a second and consider this question, "If it can be frustrating relating to a person with ADHD—how difficult can it be to actually live that way?"

Attention and concentration problems can become a driving force not only for the person with ADHD but also for those who are close to him or her. In some cases families begin to label a child with ADHD as "lazy," "troubled," or an "instigator." In reality, although kids can make bad decisions and cause tension, many times a child with ADHD acts the way he or she does because they have no choice. ADHD is a medical condition just like diabetes, depression, or arthritis. You would not get down on a person with a physical disability simply because, "Every day, without fail, you have trouble walking!" Of course, such a situation crosses the border into ludicrous behavior. Yet, many people, both within families and in "helping profession" sometimes label children with attention problems in negative ways.

In your own family, classroom, or school it is essential to understand the rules of the game when dealing with youngsters identified as having ADHD. Just like in the age old game of chess, so too in coping with these interpersonal needs there are some strategies and tactics that will be more beneficial than others. In a way it is possible to achieve a checkmate or "win" the game of life by working with rather than against the needs of a child or adolescent with Attention Deficit Disorder. What follows are some of the main supports that can be put into place when trying to successfully help these distracted yet infinitely valuable children & youths.

A. **Behave in a Loving Way:** Naturally, the vast majority of parents believe that they are acting in a loving manner. However, if you find yourself always dishing out punishments and finding your parental role an overwhelming one, you may need to step back for a bit and reassess what you are doing. A child who acts impulsively, struggles in school, has difficulties in social situations, and makes poor choices can be maddening. But, that child is your son, daughter, or student. If you try to act in a way to bespeak your compassion and love of that child, you will generally make far better decisions than otherwise. When you reach a frustration point with a youngster with ADHD stop for a few seconds, breath deeply, and recall the fact that you care about this young person. You may be called upon to be firm and corrective in your actions as an authority figure, but you cannot go wrong if you always come back to your core value of love.

B. **Try to be Non-Judgmental:** Your distracted son sits down at the dinner table. You have had a hard day at work and your patience is thin. Almost immediately, your son impulsively reaches across his sister's plate, grabs the milk, and proceeds to spill not only his own glass of soda but his sister's sixteen ounces of milk all over the family meal. You respond to this mistake by immediately yelling at him, "Greg, you are the stupidest thing on two feet. Can't you ever do anything right. My God, don't you realize what a mess you've made? Get out of my sight." What lessons have been taught in this situation? Do we really want our own son to think he is the stupidest person in the world? Will an encounter like this improve family relationships? Are we punishing our own child, at least in part, for what a mediocre time we had at work? Appropriate consequences for bad actions are an essential part of parenting or teaching. But, when we personalize our judgments we cross a line and become destructive. Refrain from judging others and you may not be judged harshly yourself. Keep cool and deal with problems rather than labeling people.

C. **Become Counter Intuitive:** In many cases youngsters with ADHD will act and then think. In some of those circumstances when you ask the child later why they did something that ended up working out badly for them they may quite honestly say, "I really don't know." This kind of non-reflective behavior is one of the worst elements of ADHD. Therefore, you need to be adept at figuring out when a child with ADHD's actions were willful and when they were so impulsive that they can only be described as a reflex. If you think the child's actions were reflexive rather than premeditated, match your response to that fact. Let the youngster know what they should or could have done instead of their unsuccessful actions, and be fair in your own responses. Some people in your family or who you work with may question your actions and state, "That's not fair—why does Greg get away with things that others don't?" But, that sort of normalized thinking is unfair in and of itself. Be counter intuitive and balance the realities of the world with the fact that the youngster has a disability that warrants consideration and instruction.

D. **Use Mentoring Opportunities**: Sometimes the biggest favor you can do for a youngster with ADHD is to recognize that someone else may be better at helping them with a certain facet of their life & learning than you are. This can be a very difficult admission for a loving parent or a proud teacher. However, facts are facts—you cannot hit a homerun with every problem. For example, if you are a single mother trying to raise a son with ADHD and getting your son to do homework is becoming a serious problem in your relationship with your child, try to find help. Perhaps the school has an after-hours homework club. Maybe your church or a local community agency has a tutoring program. Check to see if your son's school has any partnerships with community groups to provide in school tutoring. Look into community organizations that offer "big brother" programs or community mentors. Your search may be fruitless or it could result in a mentoring relationship in your son's life that not only helps him but also eases the pressures that can build up in a conflict-laden family.

E. **Assess, Accept, & Welcome Friendships:** Making friends can be one of the saddest areas of a child with ADHD's life. The ability to read social cues, concentrate in games, behave in a way that makes others want to play with you, and even have the judgment to pick realistic friends are all trouble spots for many youngsters with ADHD. Therefore, if your son or daughter is making any progress in the friendship game take time to get to know something about his or her friends. If the relationship is one that will be very destructive for your child you have to intervene. However, if your son or daughter has the makings of a friendship, do everything you can to encourage it. Make your home "kid friendly" so that your child and his friend or friends can have a place to play video games, talk, watch movies, or just hang out in a reasonable way. Get to know some things about your child's friends. Encourage your child to have his or her friends over to your home. In that way your child is validated and he or she sees that you understand how important friends are in the world. Also, the more opportunity you have to directly supervise your child's world the better you will know it. Do not be surprised if your son or daughter who has ADHD ends up with friends who have ADHD. This is not an uncommon scenario. Although that can make for some wild times consider the isolating alternative and the loneliness that it will impose on your child.

F. **Be Patient:** One of the most important yet challenging aspects of parenting or teaching children with ADHD is the way in which they can try an adult's patience. The student who has to constantly raise their hand or blurt out information can drive you crazy if you let them. In families, always having hours of homework that is a struggle to get through can become exhausting. If you live with or teach a child with ADHD you will have to face a hard fact—it will be harder for them to act in a way that they & you wish they could. If you are impatient with the symptoms of their disability you will only reduce their self-esteem, create stress for yourself and the young-ster, and damage the relationship. Hard though it may be, in patience lie the seeds of hope. In impatience lie the seeds of alienation.

G. **Recognize Conflict Cycles:** Imagine this scenario, every morning your spouse has the responsibility of making sure your son who has ADHD gets his school materials together and gets off to school on time. Every morning these seemingly simple tasks end up with an argument, yelling, door slamming, and conflict. How long can that go on before damage is done? If there is a consistent conflict cycle in your relationship with anyone you need to set aside time to reflect on both the reality of that cycle and how to break it. When we acknowledge conflict cycles we take the first step in working around or through them. In this example perhaps the other spouse should be the person responsible for handling those morning organizational chores. Maybe all that is needed is to teach your son how to use an alarm clock and how to organize his materials himself. Try something different and work as a team rather than as a group of balky horses each pulling in a different direction and unwilling to change their habits.

H. Avoid Hot Buttons: Most people have certain words, deeds, or actions that they know can set off another person. When times get tough sometimes those "hot buttons" get pushed just to get even, because its fun, or due to anger. If you are always either pushing your child with ADHD's "hot buttons" or having your own pushed by him or her—stop and think about what you are doing. For example, if your daughter who has been identified with ADHD goes to weekly counseling sessions aimed at helping her understand and cope with her disability and she is reluctant to attend, it is very probable that tension will mount as you drive her to or from the session. Therefore, either arrange transportation so that you are not solely doing it or adopt a strategy of quiet listening when you are in the car. The innocent question, "How was your therapy session today?" may result in a major brawl. Learn from the mistakes of the past—discover the hot buttons—then leave them alone or deactivate them.

I. Emphasize Openness: If you listen more than speaking you may actually hear some things. If you watch instead of staring at the television you might see things about your family that could otherwise be missed. By being open to the people around you life actually deepens. If your son with ADHD asks you to come watch him play a video game put aside what you are doing and spend some time with him. It does not matter if you have any real interest or understanding of the game. You are not really going to watch the game—no, you are going to share time with your child. If your children learn that they can come to you and actually talk to you without being ignored, devalued, or judged they will seek you out.

If, on the other hand, you are a closed door in their lives—what can you expect?

J. **Modeling is Vital:** What we say is important—What we do is vital. An adult who lectures a child about compassion and then acts in a cruel way to others teaches a terrible lesson of hypocrisy. Perhaps no element of teaching is more important than modeling. Think back to a teacher or person whom you respect. Why do you respect them? If you really think about it your respect probably flows from the way that person treated you. That memory of respect is an example of the power of modeling. So, when helping a youngster with ADHD you must remember the powerful messages you send with your actions.

K. **Value Closeness:** How would you feel if after accomplishing something very important to you at work you came home and not one single person in your family even listened to you when you shared that good news? It is quite possible that such a situation could be very deflating. Remember that fact and apply the lesson to your interactions with children with ADHD. Even though such a youngster can be difficult to cope with they are a unique and worthy individual. The time you spend with that child—the effort you pour into the relationship—cannot be measured in terms of value. Value closeness—emphasize sharing—make time available.

L. **Set Clear Expectations:** For a youngster with ADHD life can be confusing enough without adults being unclear. When setting standards for a youngster with ADHD be sure they are clear, understood, and achievable. For example, do not say, "Well, if you rake the front yard today something good might happen." No, be specific and clear by saying, "John, I need you to rake the front yard this morning. If you finish it by 10:00 we can go fishing this afternoon." Think of your own life and ask yourself, "Do I like it when things are vague and uncertain?" If the answer is no, then for heavens sake do not make things vague and unclear for a youngster who already has difficulty reading the environment.

M. Use Natural & Proportional Consequences: If you make a single mistake at work you probably do not deserve to be fired. Likewise, every time your child with ADHD makes a mistake they, too, do not deserve to have the ceiling drop on them. Consequences are a part of life. We all face consequences every day of our lives. If we exceed the speed limit when a police officer is around we run the risk of getting a ticket. If we insult our boss' intelligence we may have to look for another job. But, by and large, the consequences we give and receive should be fair. As a parent or teacher it is essential that you match reasonable consequences that are natural and proportional to a child's actions. For example, you would not expel a child from school for failing to complete homework. So too, in families, punishments or consequences need to be reasonable. When, for example, we say to a child, "You're going to be grounded for life," we make two fundamental mistakes. First, the punishment is obviously unreasonable and never going to happen. Second, it is an overreaction that can only be destructive. Both rewards and punishments need to be on par with the behaviors that call for them. This is a cardinal rule of behavioral psychology and it is a good one to remember.

In closing, the ideas and suggestions above are in no way "magic bullets" that will cure your child's ADHD. However, these types of thoughts can act to make your relationship with that youngster much more fulfilling. How can you hope to establish a relationship of value with a person you really do not understand or spend time with? By using some thought about how you behave with a child you can deepen that rapport. Hopefully some of these ideas will ring true with you or cause you to at least think about how you are relating to a child.

8.

Preparing For Staffings:
10 Tips For Parents & Educators

Staffings are designed to be problem-solving meetings. In theory, all participants come to a staffing with information, knowledge, or general input aimed at designing an effective educational program for a child. However, in some cases, staffings become discordant sessions laced with conflict. In order to avoid this negative outcome it may be valuable to think about some basic strategies aimed at making a staffing a source of problem resolution and not one of anger, frustration, and conflict. Providing such strategies to parents prior to a meeting is an act of moral leadership on the part of educators and may act to cement a partnership with an otherwise oppositional family. Listed below are ten relatively common sense approaches that may be helpful in preparing for and participating in a child's staffing.

1. **READ YOUR RIGHTS:** At any sort of staffing, pre-referral meeting, or evaluation session the school district staff are responsible for providing you with a copy of your rights in brief. Take the time to read through those rights and highlight any sections that you believe apply to your child. If, after reading your child's educational rights, you feel that something is wrong be sure to contact the appropriate school representative and discuss it. For example, if you receive the required notice of your

child's staffing and the regular classroom teacher has been left uninvited please be sure to communicate the necessity of that person's attendance to the relevant party. Know what you and your child are legally entitled to and respectfully advocate for it.

2. **ASK QUESTIONS THROUGHOUT THE PROCESS:** At any time that you feel there are points that are unclear or if you are concerned about what is being said or left unsaid be confident enough to ask questions. Yes, it can be intimidating to speak out in a meeting with a relatively large number of school professionals but always remember that you have the longest standing relationship with your child. Make sure that people use language, which you understand. There are times when professionals fall into a form of jargon that can be confusing. Always be sure to request a clarification of points that seem vague to you. In such instances you probably are not the only person at the table figuratively scratching their head and wondering what something meant.

3. **WRITE THINGS DOWN:** Before you go to the staffing prepare a list of keynote questions or points that you want to be sure are addressed. Keep a pad of paper near your bed, post a post-it note on the refrigerator, or keep a note pad by the telephone in order to capture the key issues you want covered at the meeting. During the meeting check off those points as they are presented. Hopefully, all your concerns will come to light via the school staff during the course of the staffing. However, if something does not come up you have your list of concerns to refer to and bring up. By writing things down you provide yourself with a reminder list for the staffing. Most people do not go the grocery store without a list. Why would you go to your child's educational planning or evaluation meeting without one?

4. ASK FOR TEST RESULTS AHEAD OF TIME: In some instances diagnostic staff such as psychologists are very strapped for time. In those circumstances they will probably not be able to get you a report summary prior to the staffing. However, that is not always the case and it certainly hurts nobody to make a request for such information before the meeting. Having assessment results prior to the staffing will help you to mentally and emotionally prepare for the meeting. If, for example, this is your child's three-year reevaluation it might be beneficial to know what achievement scores are ahead of time. In cases when it is an initial evaluation meeting it certainly could assist a parent to know whether or not there is a probability that the test data will point toward a learning disability. Knowledge is strength and can help you to be stronger and more productive in a meeting. You probably would not go to take a test without at least some study. Having this type of assessment information ahead of time allows you to study and prepare for your child's meeting.

5. ASK FOR RESOURCE INFORMATION: When you are meeting with educational professionals take advantage of their expertise. If, for example, the staff are talking about issues such as language development, auditory learning, sensory regulation, or any number of other complex issues of information processing be sure to request whatever resource information they can provide. Also be aware that we live in an information age. Simply by logging on to a computer and surfing the web you can in virtually seconds access information that, in previous years, would have been inaccessible to you. Learn everything that you can about your child's disability or potential needs. By preparing and researching you will become both more comfortable in meetings and a better advocate for your child.

6. **PROVIDE STAFF WITH EVALUATION INFORMATION:**
   Often parents of children with disabilities or perceived needs will have already been involved with other professionals or clinicians prior to their coming to school. If your family has already undertaken independent assessments with neurologists, psychiatrists, speech pathologists, developmental therapists, or any other evaluator you should provide that data to the school personnel before you meet with them. A true "team effort" requires all parties focusing upon a shared goal. In the case of a staffing that focus must be upon the child. In order to make the best team decision sharing information is essential.

7. **ADOPT A POSITIVE PROBLEM-SOLVING MODE:**
   Staffings can become very tense. Parents and school staff can be nervous and stressed before, during, and after a complex IEP meeting. However, if you can adopt an attitude of group commitment and problem solving it will cut through these negative emotions. Yes, you may not be able to come to an agreement with the school personnel on every issue but, if you are open to reasonable compromise and negotiation you stand a far greater chance of having not only one but a long sequence of positive meetings with the school people.

8. **GAUGE YOUR OWN EMOTIONS:** It can be highly challenging to read your own emotions when you feel stressed. Parents can come into staffings feeling anger, frustration, pain, fear, and a host of other sensations. If you can measure your own emotional pulse during a processing meeting you place yourself in a better position to be productive. If you feel that it is too difficult to do so be sure that your spouse or another trusted person is there to help you by monitoring not only what happens at the staffing but also how you handled things.

Emotions are a natural and productive aspect of live. Yet, emotions unchecked by reason can lead to pain and anguish.

9. **DO NOT JUDGE PEOPLE BY THEIR BODY LANGUAGE:** Reading the body language of the members of a group is an essential skill for any meeting facilitator. People communicate a great deal by how they sit, their physical mannerisms, or where they sit. Try to be aware of these things when you attend your child's staffing. However, do not read too much into any one behavior. The person who may appear defensive at the meeting could, in fact, merely be nervous. A person seemingly on the fringe of a meeting may actually be shy or simply a good listener. By being observant yet non-judgmental of how people act at your child's staffing you may develop a deeper understanding of what actually transpired.

10. **BRING A SUPPORT PERSON IF NEEDED:** As was noted above having a person you trust at a staffing can be a great benefit. Often, people who are going to a significant medical consultation are advised to have a loved one come along with them. The tension or anxiety inherent in such a meeting is obvious. By having a caring person at your side you have a better guarantee that what is said will be heard. You may simply be too emotionally involved to accurately understand what is happening. Further, in a staffing there are many complicated and potentially litigious issues that may come up. While you may be a well-informed parent as per your child's educational rights under the Individuals with Disabilities Education Act or section 504 you might benefit from having an advocate or expert support person at your side. In other instances by merely having your spouse or a friend at the meeting you arm yourself with greater emotional support. In some instances your support person may be a school staff member whom you have faith in.

Whatever the unique circumstances never hesitate to seek out whatever type of support you feel you need prior to the staffing. Public advocacy groups or information sites on the web can provide you with reasonable support.

In closing, it is a truism to state that parent's sometimes come to staffings with points of contention, fear, anger, or confusion inside of themselves. Additionally, school staff can also come to such meetings tense and on edge. By adopting some of the strategies listed above it can be possible to hold staffings that are child centered and well focused. The role of the school staff is to provide a Free and Appropriate Public Education (FAPE) to each child with a disability. In a very real sense that is an almost sacred trust. While many professionals take that commitment seriously some do not. If you can come to your child's meeting armed with both information and reason you place your child's interest in greater trust. Hopefully, through preparation, reflection, and fairness you can leave each staffing feeling that not only have your child's needs been addressed but also that you are working with an educational institution with a human face. If that noble goal can be accomplished then everyone prospers.

9.

What Can I Expect from the School—
Section 504 & Special Education

If your child with ADD is experiencing serious problems in the classroom you may well find yourself asking for some form of assessment and help from school officials. If you feel that your child's ADD is affecting his or her learning in a noteworthy way then you should be aware of the rights and responsibilities that are in operation due to his or her disability. When looking for specific help for your child from the school, you are entering into a field governed by a series of laws, regulations, and procedural safeguards. You are also entering into an area where there are two primary avenues for getting help for your child—Section 504 & Special Education.

Both Section 504 and special education are pathways that can be followed to create support plans, inclusive of a wide variety of accommodations, for your child with ADD. Section 504 and special education are related but far different in terms of the scope of services that can be brought to bear for your child's benefit. In looking at ways and means that can be grasped in pursuit of assisting your child's learning it is important to generally understand the differences between 504 and special education. Listed below is a very brief summary of the cardinal factors involved in both 504 & special education

- Section 504 – An outgrowth of civil rights legislation of the 1970's, Section 504 calls for reasonable accommodations to critical life activities and access for people with identified disabilities. Under 504, agencies that receive Federal funds must assure that equal access is available to all reasonable participants. For example, a public library must be sure that it has curve cuts, handicap accessible bathroom facilities, and some way of allowing for access to individuals with physical disabilities. A failure to do so would be a violation of Section 504 and could result in legal action, sanctions, court awards in civil cases, and a withdrawal of Federal funding. In schools, learning is defined as a critical life activity and can result in the need to develop an accommodation plan due to a child's disability. That accommodation plan would have to include "reasonable accommodations to general education" in order to address the child's identified disability. Later in this chapter a listing of typical 504 accommodations is included.

- Special Education – Since the early 1970's a series of Federal and state laws have been crafted each of which defines the need to provide "Free and Appropriate Public Education" (FAPE) to children who have been identified as having a significant disability that affects learning. The most important law governing special education practices and requirements is the Federal Individuals with Disabilities Education Act (IDEA). This Federal law is massive in nature and has been reauthorized by Congress and the Whitehouse several times over the years. While far too extensive to adequately summarize in this booklet, IDEA provides a vast road map touching on areas such as testing, child identification, educational services, funding, parental rights, due process, and the nature of FAPE. Under special education law once a child has been referred for evaluation for a potential disability and his or her parent or guardian has provided written consent for specific evaluations in specific domains, the district must complete the assessment in 60 school days and, if the child qualifies for services, develop an Individual Education Plan (IEP) that maps out services and means of measuring student progress. Under IDEA students eligible for special education may access a wide range of potentially comprehensive services at district expense. Where Section 504 calls for "reasonable accommodations to general education" IDEA requires an "appropriate education" aimed at meeting the student's needs. Special education is far more comprehensive in its scope than 504 and requires much more resource allocation on the part of the school district.

In considering a potential evaluation by your child's school district you should bear several points in mind. Among the most important are:

1. How severe are your child's educational needs? The more severe the more likely you should be leaning toward special education versus 504.

2. How open is the school district to helping you? The more adversarial or uncooperative the district is, the more unlikely it is that they will responsibly follow the looser guidelines of 504 versus special education.

3. How open is your child to receiving specialized help? If your child is adamantly opposed to accepting any extra help that attitude might be a roadblock to progress and could cause you to hesitate in going forward with a school district assessment.

4. What do your professional support people think? What are the opinions of your child's doctor, counselor, minister, or

tutor regarding a potential evaluation and services? If they feel strongly ask them to provide you a letter stating their credentials and opinions. Then include a copy of that correspondence with your referral to the district for an assessment. Expert testimony can be very helpful as you work with the district.

5. How stressful has your child's school performance been to your entire family? If your son or daughter is struggling and the cost to the child and your entire family is high, do not hesitate and approach the school district asking for help.

6. How significant are your child's school problems? If, for example, your child's grades are OK but he or she struggles with homework, then you probably want to consider a 504 route with the focus being on accommodations linked to homework. On the other hand, if your child is failing at school and demonstrating behavioral and emotional problems, then the stakes are much higher and a special education evaluation is more appropriate.

7. What were your own school experiences like? Without projecting your own experience onto your child, take some time and think back to what school was like for you when you were younger. If you struggled with reading or attention in school you probably can still remember how it felt to be in class every day facing those issues. If so, then be sure to ask the district for help so that your child does not have the same sorts of memories when he or she grows up.

8. What do I have to do to get the process going? While procedures vary from district-to-district and state-to-state, in general there are some commonalities that exist due to Federal law. If you want your child evaluated for either a 504 accommodation plan or under IDEA you should contact the school principal and

discuss your wishes. Follow up that discussion with a written request for an evaluation. Include in that letter your name, your child's name, the reasons you are making the request, and the date. Providing a written request provides you documentation, stresses the seriousness of your request, and begins a clock ticking regarding the assessment time lines that the district must abide by. Be sure your letter is sent to the right person in the district. In some cases writing the principal is enough—in others you will need to send your request for testing to the director of special education or some such official. Be sure you know who to write to and what his or her address is.

9. What if the school district ignores my request? If you do not hear back from the school district in a week or two call the person you wrote and stress the need for action. The district cannot legally ignore your referral. They must at least meet with you in order to discuss the reasonableness of your request. At that meeting, if your child's needs are not that serious, the district may justifiably refuse to carry out an assessment. If so, they must provide to you in writing their rationales for not testing your child. However, if the school district simply stonewalls you and ignores your request you have every right to write to the district requesting a due process hearing to clear up the matter.

10. What is a due process hearing? Hopefully you will never be involved in a due process hearing but, if the district is adamant about either ignoring your request for assessment, or refusing to serve your child, you can request such a hearing. In that case the state department of education will appoint an impartial hearing officer who will schedule a meeting between you and your support people and the school district. Such hearings can be adversarial and often involve legal counsel. In a majority of cases hearing officers support parental claims. However this is

a tense process and one to be avoided unless as a last resort. In some states mediation can also be requested. In that process a state appointed intermediary would meet with you and district officials to try to come to a reasonable compromise.

11. Can I submit my own evaluations? Yes, you can provide the district with copies of your child's medical, psychological, psychiatric or other independent evaluations you have had completed over the years. In the case of 504 many districts will simply accept those diagnoses of the presenting problem(s) and will build a plan based upon those findings. For example, if you make a 504 referral and provide the district with a copy of the assessment that identified your child as having ADD, it is exceedingly unlikely that the school district will question those results. Conversely, if you make a special education referral and present the district with an independent psychiatric evaluation that recommends that your child be placed in a private school for children with learning disabilities that costs $25,000 per year, the district will probably oppose the use of that evaluation. Remember, if the district accepts your independent evaluation and makes use of it in the process they also must accept the recommendations contained within the plan.

As you can tell from the information included above, both 504 and IDEA are processes that include a tremendous amount of procedure and bureaucracy. Special education services can be very expensive and many school districts are facing serious financial difficulties. Therefore, school administrators may be cautious in making commitments as per your child's needs. However, within reason, your concerns must be focused upon your child's needs and not those of the school system. If your child is entitled to and requires specific services, supports, or programming it is the responsibility of the school district to provide them. Your child's welfare and legitimate needs should not be swept under the carpet because the district either does not wish to recognize them or falters in providing the legally required assistance he or she deserves.

Now, let's take a look at a series of three sample case studies. Each of these three scenarios has been drawn from real life cases with the names and events slightly altered to protect confidentiality. In each instance the result is different due to many factors. In looking at these three case studies perhaps the reader can get a practical understanding of the differences between 504, special education, and a situation wherein no services are warranted.

CASE STUDY 1 – JOHN

John is a fifth grader whose teachers thought of him as bright and reasonably sociable. Over the years John had done reasonably well in school and earned grades that typically clustered around a C level. However, John had consistently struggled to pay attention in class. John's desk was a disaster and he frequently lost homework assignments. John's parents were cooperative and both the family and school officials were often frustrated by his disorganization. In fifth grade John was falling behind in his studies. His test scores were dropping and John was even more disruptive in class than in prior years. Also, John was beginning to "shut down" at home when it came time to do homework. More and more time was being spent at home on homework and the stress in the family was growing. At school John was beginning to withdraw from some of his classmates and even had a few discipline referrals. John's teachers saw him as a bright boy with reasonable academic skills but who was just more and more unfocused. Recently John's parents had him evaluated by a local psychologist and he was identified as ADD. John had been taking 10-

mg. of Adderol in a time-release form for the past month. Finally, the family made a referral and John underwent a full evaluation inclusive of psychological testing, a social development study, and a medical review by the school nurse.

Results: At the staffing John was not found eligible for special education because his academic scores were still at grade level. The school psychologist noted that John had average ability but also was very distractible. While John's grades had dipped he still was not failing any classes. The school social worker noted that John was worried about his performance at school and the struggles it was causing. John's teachers stressed their desire to help John. In the end the team developed a 504 accommodation plan that featured:

a. Modified homework expectations that allowed John and his parents some leeway in terms of due dates and the amount of work expected of him on a daily basis.

b. John was provided a second set of textbooks to keep at home because he frequently forgot to bring needed materials home.

c. John was provided extended time to do tests so that he could concentrate.

d. The school nurse agreed to periodically observe John and report to his family so that a measure of his classroom focus could be provided to the treating physicians.

e. John was provided with a weekly counseling session with the school social worker to discuss the stress he was feeling.

f. The team agreed to meet again in six months at the latest, or earlier if John's performance continued to dip, with an eye toward potential special education services if improvement was not noted.

Analysis: John did not qualify for special education because although his needs were notable they were not so far off the scale that they required the support of special education staff. A 504 plan was developed that included reasonable modifications. A safety net was constructed in case John's performance did not improve.

Case Study 2 – William

William is a third grader who has demonstrated consistent problems learning over his years at school. William has attended the same grade school since kindergarten and every year his teachers have noted serious academic and concentration problems. William struggles to attend to directions, loses materials, often blurts out in class, and has problems relating to other students on the playground. William often forgets his materials at home and virtually never completes homework. Sometimes on tests William can do quite well but often he fails them. William is seen as a bright youngster who is very talented in building puzzles, working with Legos, and making clay figures. When engaged in these sorts of activities William can concentrate for prolonged periods of time and be productive. However, William is reading below grade level and has started to struggle in math. About six months ago William was evaluated by a local clinic and found to have ADD. He attends counseling once a week and is on a daily dose of Concerta. William was evaluated by the school district at parent request.

Results –   The evaluation results included the psychologist's finding that William had an IQ well within the high average range. William's reading comprehension and decoding skills were about six months below grade level. In math, William demonstrated stronger reasoning skills but was beginning to slip in basic calculations. The psychologist described William as "very difficult to test" and "always in motion." Even in the one-on-one testing situation William needed to move and take breaks. The social worker indicated that William had trouble identifying who his friends were in class. William also reported having trouble sleeping and worrying about "not being very smart." William was found eligible for special education services under the label of "Other Health Impaired" due to the ways in which his ADD was impacting upon his academic and social development. An IEP was written that provided daily reading instruction in a small group as well as some support via the special education teacher in the classroom. William's tests were to be slightly modified so that he could perform in a more comfortable way. The school nurse would contact William's physician with information about his school performance. William's parents would meet with psychiatrist to discuss either a change in medication or a different dosage.

Analysis: William qualified for special education due to the severity of his school problems and the identified impact his ADD had upon learning. Since there was a measurable gap between where William was performing in reading and math and where he should have been, the team felt he was demonstrating a disability linked to his identified medical condition—ADD.

Case Study 3 – Hannah

Hannah is an eleventh grader whose grades are generally at a B level. Hannah has been privately assessed and found to have an IQ in the superior range as well as a mild incidence of ADD. Hannah's ADD does not seem to affect her in class as her teachers report that she impresses them with her study habits, test performance, organization, and timely work completion. Hannah has friends in school and is a participant in several school clubs & activities. Hannah's parents want her to go on to a four-year college and worry about her ability to score a high enough mark on the ACT to gain admission to a "good school." Recently, Hannah has earned grades in the C range on several unit tests in her American History and Spanish classes. Even though Hannah is carrying a class load that includes college prep courses and has typically done well in school without accommodation, her parents requested a full evaluation of their daughter. After at first being refused an assessment, Hannah's parents secured an attorney and "convinced" the district to evaluate Hannah. Hannah herself is quiet about potentially being "labeled."

Results – Hannah was found to have an IQ of about 115, falling in the high average range. The school psychologist reported that Hannah's academic skills all fell above average and within the range of expectations given her ability. While Hannah seemed to be mildly distractible her scores in that area did not appear to be significant. Hannah gave no evidence of having any emotional or behavioral problems. Teacher reports continued to indicate that Hannah was doing well in class and that she was a "model student." Recently, Hannah had shown improvement in the two classes where her test grades had slipped a bit. Hannah reported to the social worker that she thought her test grades had dropped because she had started dating a boy "she really liked" and that she had been temporarily "distracted" from her studies. Hannah thought school was "great" but she did feel a little pressured by her parents about choosing the "right" college to go to. None of Hannah's teachers felt she had any difficulty with timed tests or completing work in class on her own. Hannah's parents did not indicate that their daughter struggled to complete homework. Hannah was found ineligible for either special education or 504 services, as her school performance did not indicate any significant need.

Analysis: Just because a child has ADD does not mean they need support at school. Yes, in some instances school staff can be ignorant or obstructionist in regards to helping your child or even understanding his or her disability. However, if your child is able to cope with his or her ADD, do not try to force help where it is not needed. Hannah was a bright girl who was marginally underachieving. Her needs were being met and she was succeeding. Therefore, no services were warranted.

In instances where a child is found eligible for either 504 or special education services some sort of school plan will need to be written out, implemented, and monitored. If your child has an IEP there will be goals & objectives that are based upon areas of need. Specific services will be written into the plan as well as how frequently and on what basis those staff members will work with your child. Also, modifications to the curriculum, behavior planning, medical needs, or any number of other alterations to general education will be included in the plan. On a quarterly basis your child's primary special education teacher, or case manager, should provide you some brief written report as per your child's progress. On at least an annual basis there should be a formal IEP meeting where your child's progress is discussed in depth and a new plan for the following year is developed. If your child is transitioning at the end of the year to another school (e.g. and 8th grader moving on to high school) members of the receiving school staff should be included in the meeting to assure a smoother move. In every case, at the end of an IEP meeting you should receive a copy of the plan. You are a part of the team and you should act and be treated as such.

Likewise in 504 an accommodation plan should be developed inclusive of the presenting problems, the child's diagnosis, documentation of any assessments conducted, and the reasonable accommodations to general education that will be put in place and implemented. A case manager will need to be assigned and that person will act to oversee the implementation of the 504 plan. Case managers for 504 plans can be people such as the school nurse, social worker, classroom teacher, counselor, or another responsible party involved in the plan. The 504 plan needs to be revisited at a formal meeting at least once a year. 504 services cannot be dropped unless there is a formal meeting at which they are found by the team to be no longer necessary.

In terms of the types of accommodations that can be included in either 504 plans or IEP's what follows is a finite list of some typical ones for both sorts of plans. In looking at these services and modifications take note of the differences between a 504 plans and special education. Remember, a child in special education demonstrates needs that are more severe than those shown by a youngster receiving 504 services.

SAMPLE LISTING OF CLASSROOM MODIFICATIONS: 504:

1. Extra time to complete tests.

2. Second set of textbooks for home use.

3. Test taking in small groups with fewer distractions.

4. Monitoring of medication needs at school.

5. Participation in a social skills group at school.

6. Consultation with the child's counselor or doctor.

7. Homework monitoring system to assure school-home communication.

8. Inclusion in small group re-teaching groups if available.

9. Some form of classroom reinforcement system to improve concentration & behavior.

10. Extra time and/or advance notice about long-term projects.

SPECIAL EDUCATION:

1. Modified test and quizzes.

2. Alternate curriculum designed to match your child's present levels of performance and learning style.

3. Small group instruction aimed at your child's needs.

4. Supervised administration of medication at school.

5. Individual or group counseling at school.

6. Close communication with your child's medical staff to the extent you authorize it.

7. Daily or weekly communication system aimed at improving your ability to stay in touch with your child's school performance and homework/study needs.

8. Specific instruction by highly qualified special education staff in areas of need. This instruction may occur in the general class or in smaller groups.

9. Modified behavior plan that recognizes your child's disability and causes modifications to regular school discipline consequences to occur in accordance with your child's disability.

10. Curriculum and instruction designed to meet your child's needs and implemented by professionals trained in disability education.

While this limited list touches on only a few areas that could be part of either a 504 plan or an IEP, the point is hopefully made that both routes offer some form of help. Under 504 the accommodations are more circumspect. In special education the alterations can be fundamental. In any case, the level of support should be based upon your child's needs and the most reasonable way to address them.

If you feel your child is floundering at school you should approach school staff members and speak with them. Stay in close touch with your child's teacher(s). Make sure they realize what your son or daughter's needs are. Do not be afraid to contact them. Try to remember that your child is not their sole responsibility but that his or her interests are your primary concern. If you feel the need for some form of school-based assessment be sure to ask for it. Once that process is completed be sure your rights, and those of your child, are being looked after. If a plan of any sort is developed make sure it matches your child's needs. Remember that if you feel uncomfortable with the way the school district is handling your child's case you have legal and procedural recourse. Try to work cooperatively with the school system but do not shortchange your child. Do not attempt to jerry-rig or bully your way into some sort of accommodation plan if your child's needs do not warrant it. But, above all else, keep your child's legitimate needs at the forefront and be a responsible advocate for his or her welfare.

10.

ADD—FAQ's

Raising a child or children with ADD can be exhausting, perplexing, and down right hard. Days will pass when you may wonder if you will ever understand your child. On other days you will fail to be a great parent and will lose sleep over some of the things you have said and done. In a nutshell—you are not perfect and rearing children with ADD can be a supreme challenge. But even when you are at these low points remember the fact that you are not alone—you can ask questions and look for help.

What follows is a living list of commonly asked questions related to parenting children with ADD as well as our attempts to address them. Over time we will add and subtract from this section of the booklet as new and more relevant questions come to us or if changing times make others unimportant. If you have a question please feel free to contact us and we will do our best to share what we know or can find out in regards to your issue.

FREQUENTLY ASKED QUESTIONS CONCERNING PARENTING CHILDREN WITH ADD

1. **What can I do when my child is driving me crazy?** It is OK to be upset by things your child does. What is important is what you do after you realize that you are upset. It will only make things worse if you lose your temper, blow up, and create a worse

situation. Learn to recognize when you are getting upset. Try to calm or remove yourself from the situation before it escalates. Find time to get away from the situation before you lose it. Build respite time into your schedule. Go out alone or with your partner to spend time together away from the stressful home situation. Find things that your child likes to do and share them with him or her. Make your life saner and you will be healthier.

2. **How can I get my child's school to understand his/her needs?** Teachers, principals, and other school people may or may not have a good grasp of what ADD in general, and your child's version of it in particular, mean. Rather than assuming that the school staff understands your child's needs be sure to give them valuable information. Prepare a simple and concise one page profile of your child. Include in it the nature of his or her ADD, accommodations that have worked in past years, things you do at home to help with schoolwork, your child's strengths, and personal interests of your child. Make sure every teacher who works with your child has a copy of the profile. Stay in close contact with your child's teachers. Maintain a positive attitude toward the teachers. Remember, teachers are human beings too, and it is only natural that if they perceive you in a positive light, they are more likely to work cooperatively with your child.

3. **Why is my child so inconsistent at school and at home?** Children with ADD can be maddeningly inconsistent. One week they are acing their schoolwork and the next week you are getting notes form teachers asking why so many homework assignments are missing. ADD is a condition that breeds inconsistency. Frustrating though it may be try not to take these peaks and valleys of performance personally. Instead of blowing up when things go bad stress having systems in place. For example, if your child is erratic in terms of homework completion, be sure

that you have a daily monitoring system in place that you & your child's teachers check. In this way there is an external structure in place to support your child when he or she falters. Over time greater independence should be the goal but, until your child demonstrates the ability to handle that sort of independence, external structures & systems act as insurance policies.

4. **Why doesn't my child have friends?** Making friends is a complicated process requiring solid social skills. All too often children with ADD behave in ways that drive off potential friends. The child who disrupts a board game by grabbing pieces or skipping turns will get on other kids' nerves. Likewise, an impulsive person may behave in ways that are unpredictable. Unpredictability is a major barrier in the development of positive and meaningful social relationships. For your child to develop friendships requires that he or she is being treated appropriately and, thereby, is demonstrating social skills that welcome other people into his or her life. The key to friendships lies in your child's ability to model behaviors that make it less risky for other people to open up their lives to him or her. Social skills can be taught but the key rests in helping your child to develop and maintain a healthy self-concept that is based upon improvement in major life areas. Then friendships that are supportive, pro-social, and fulfilling can occur.

5. **Are there any support services available at the college level?** Yes, although such services are far less comprehensive than those available in grades K-12 they exist nonetheless. Remember that under Section 504 agencies accepting Federal funding must have procedures and services in place to allow access for individuals with disabilities. At the college level such access infers the availability of some form of accommodation due to recognized disabilities. Therefore, if a youngster has ADD he or

she can access certain modifications and supports at the college's expense. For example, if your son or daughter contacts the college's department that deals with such accommodations and presents them with proof of his or her disability some supports will need to be provided. Examples of such supports could be the ability to take tests in a learning lab with a computer, extended time on major projects, access to counseling services, or tutorial services. While the supports may vary from one college or junior college to another, the fact remains that some sort of accommodation is required so long as your child asks for it & can verify that he or she actually has a disability.

6. **How can my college-aged child verify their disability?** When you attend school meetings, IEP staffings, or 504 accommodation planning meetings you will generally receive some sort of paperwork. Always keep those forms and maintain a record of your child's services. When the time comes for your child to approach the college's department of disability supports or access, he or she should bring with the most recent evaluation report, IEP, or 504 plan in order to validate his or her claim. In addition, if you have recent medical reports that verify your child's ADD make sure copies of those are available in case the university staff request further information. If you do not have any of the school forms have your child contact the district and request a copy of those records. Special education and 504 records are temporary school documents and will be maintained by the district for five years after the time your child graduates from high school. After that time period has lapsed those records will be destroyed so be sure you have what you need prior to that time period sun setting.

7. **Will my child's ADD ever go away?** There really is no way to definitively answer this question. In many instances ADD

will remain a factor in a person's life forever. Stop and think, if ADD is a legitimate medical condition why would it sun set. Of course, like other medical conditions that respond well to treatment, ADD can be controlled and channeled but will it disappear—probably not. That fact does not mean that a person's ADD needs to be a burden to them throughout their life. Certainly not as ADD under control can translate to descriptors like "high energy," "highly productive," "a real go-getter," and "tireless." If a person's ADD is treated and understood it need not be a barrier to any sort of happiness or success. For example, during the American Civil War General William Tecumseh Sherman was at various times described as fidgety, always in motion, sleepless, a rapid-fire & non-stop talker, a person who always blurted out ideas, and depressed. General Sherman was ADD at a time when people were more than a century away from even knowing what those letters meant. William Tecumseh Sherman was also one of the most successful military leaders, public speakers, and wits of his or any other era in American history. People with ADD can be immensely successful if they can channel their talents into the right fields.

8. **Is ADD a genetic disorder & will my grandchildren be ADD?** There is research that indicates that ADD can run in families and most often is passed on from the paternal side. Therefore, although it is not definitely true in all cases, there is enough evidence to indicate that children with ADD frequently have parents or other relatives who manifest the same symptoms. Carrying on with that thought, it is also possible that your grandchildren may also manifest some of those symptoms as well. Thus, it is doubly important that you seek out and maintain positive treatment for your child's ADD. If your son or daughter has ADD and could potentially be a parent to children who could be ADD, would it not be

best to make sure that your child's condition is under control before they become a parent? Consider this scenario, you ignore or punish your child's ADD and then they, in turn, become parents of children with ADD. How prepared will your child be to raise a child with ADD? There is no guarantee that your grandchildren will develop ADD, but do you not want them to have the greatest possible chance of happiness? If so, then take your child's needs seriously and do everything you can to positively treat them so that they are as prepared as they can be to become positive and nurturing parents themselves.

9. **My son always forgets to do the things I ask him to do, is this part of his ADD?** It may or may not be but you should bear in mind that ADD can affect processing speed, memory, and recall. Sometimes kids "selectively remember" things you tell them. The chores they did not want to do are conveniently "forgotten." However, in many instances a child with ADD will simply be unable to process or remember directions. For example, you ask your son to go upstairs, get his math book, and bring down the dirty dishes from his room. A few minutes later your son comes back downstairs with his book and asks, "What was it you wanted upstairs?" In this situation it is quite possible that your son really never "heard" you when you first asked him to go upstairs and do those things. Try to be patient and ask your son or daughter to repeat back to you what is expected of them. If you want them to accomplish two things be sure they can tell you what those two things are. In this way you increase the likelihood of your child actually remembering at least one of the two requests.

10. **Is my child ADD or just lazy?** In all of the English language there may not be a more powerful word than "lazy." When we call someone lazy we judge them to be essentially worthless.

Many times adults look at a child's behavior and label it as lazy. When they do this they erect an almost unbreakable barrier between themselves and that child. A child with ADD may be working incredibly hard and still fail. Just because they miss assignments, lose papers, misplace materials, or do poorly on tests does not mean that they are not trying. In fact, think how frustrating it must be to try so hard, fail, and then be told you are lazy. In fact, that type of situation could be heartbreaking. It is almost never right to call a child, or an adult, lazy. That word carries so much power that it will leave a stain on the relationship of the giver and receiver of it.

11. **Should I help my child with his/her homework or should I make them become independent?** When your child is capable of working independently and succeeding then let them. If your child needs help & guidance with their homework do so. If you have to type your child's book report while he or she dictates it to you go ahead and be sure to inform the teacher of what you are doing. If your child cannot prepare for tests without your help, study with them. Approach your child's schoolwork as a process rather than an event. When your son or daughter shows gains recognize them and back off a bit. But, even when your child is becoming more independent be sure to keep tabs on how they are doing at school. You really do not want surprises at mid-term progress report time, on report cards, or at parent-teacher meetings.

12. **I think my child has a learning disability along with ADD—what should I do?** First, understand what a learning disability is. In school terms a learning disability (LD) exists when a child has average or above ability and a significant delay in one or more key achievement domain that is not the direct result of a medical, environmental, sensory, linguistic,

or mobility factor. In lay terms, this translates to a child with an IQ in the average or above range who has an achievement gap that is statistically significant and that is not due to factors other than learning processes. The gap in achievement varies depending upon the age of the child. For example, at the lower elementary grades a one-year discrepancy between ability and achievement is significant. In middle school the achievement gap would have to be greater than two years to achieve significance. In high school a gap of more than three years is necessary for statistical significance to be reached. Also, the learning problems your child is experiencing need to be unrelated to any medical factors inclusive of ADD. Thus, if you suspect a learning disability you should assess your child's performance and see if the gaps exist and that the problems go beyond the needs created by your child's ADD. Symptoms of a learning disability beyond the achievement gaps may also include factors such as reversals, mirror writing, poor visual-motor coordination, and extreme memory/comprehension deficits. If you feel your child may have an LD problem contact the school and request an evaluation of your child. Remember, it is possible to have more than one disability and there are a number of children who are identified as eligible for special education services with both health needs and LD concerns.

13. **My son has gotten into significant discipline problems at school and the district wants to expel him---what can I do?**
To begin, it may well be permissible for a school district to expel a child with ADD. However, before they can do so the district must first assess your child's behavior in light of his disability. If the actions your child undertook are causally related to his disability then an expulsion cannot occur. Naturally, in such a situation the district may seek to change your son's educational placement due to behavioral issues but that is a separate process.

In cases like this when the child has a 504 plan or IEP, the district must conduct a "manifestation meeting" to determine the interaction between your child's ADD and his actions. For example, assume that your son with ADD has an IEP. Then assume that at dismissal time from the high school he attends, while driving out of the parking lot sitting in the back seat of a friend's car, your son impulsively grabbed a paintball gun and waved it out of the rear window. The district intends to expel your son for having a "Look alike" weapon on campus. An IEP meeting is called at which a manifestation determination will occur to assess the connection between your son's behavior and his ADD. Is what he did directly related to his condition? If so—in what ways? If not—why not? If it is unrelated and your son is expelled he is still entitled to school services. Unlike youngsters without disabilities, those with IEP's or 504 plans must continue to receive an education after expulsion. However, and bear this in mind, if your child has impulsive tendencies, there are very few behaviors that could not be interpreted as having something to do with impulsivity. Just remember that you and your son are entitled to due process. If that right is honored then the results will be equitable. If not, be sure to solicit some sort of legal or advocacy support in order to protect them.

14. **My son's teacher told me that she could not teach him unless we had him evaluated for ADD—does the district have to pay for this evaluation?** If a representative of the school has informed you that your son's education cannot be provided unless you assess him for ADD, I would first request that statement in writing. If the district is so imprudent as to provide you with a written version of the statement then the school district can be charged for the evaluation. Whenever a district indicates that an assessment is necessary for the child's education they are responsible for the cost of it. If, on the

other hand, the school staff advises that you might benefit from such an evaluation, then they are not responsible for the cost. The key factor here is when school district staff members say they must have assessment information to provide a reasonable education; they become responsible for the cost.

15. My daughter's school refuses to test her for special education because they say ADD is not a disability area—what can I do? Yes, ADD is not a specific disability category under special education law. However, the categories of "Other Health Impaired," "Learning Disability," and "Emotionally Disturbed" all are ones that some children with ADD may qualify for services under. The key rests in the amount of academic impact your child's ADD condition exerts upon learning. If your child is experiencing significant learning and/or behavioral problems at school there is a basis for first conducting an evaluation and then potentially developing an IEP under the auspices of one of the aforementioned disability categories. If the district is relying upon the absence of a separate ADD category to refuse your child an evaluation and potential services they are both stonewalling and violating the law.

16. I feel so isolated as the parent of a child with ADD—are there other people in my shoes? Parenting a child with a disability can be exhausting and isolating. Yet, you are not alone. There are millions of children in the United States who demonstrate some sort of disability. In fact, between 12-14% of all school-aged children in the United States receive some sort of special education support. Likewise, there are millions of Americans who either have ADD or are related to people who do. If you are feeling isolated consult an organization that specializes in ADD and look into any local or regional parent support groups. Similarly, local mental health sites may have support groups for parents of children with ADD. Contact the parents of other children with ADD and look into establishing a support group of your own. Make good use of your friends and family as an intimate support network. Seek out family counseling or individual counseling to talk over your needs. Stay close to your partner so that you have a loving support base in your home. Use the Internet to find resources, supports, and ideas that make life more bearable. Do not wallow in your isolation but rather look for natural supports that can enhance your life and make you both a better parent and a more complete person.

17. Should I read and study about ADD? Imagine this scenario; you are having lunch with a good friend and he tells you how upset his wife is at him for not reading about the serious health condition she suffers from. Your friend is a decent person but he simply feels that anything he needs to know about his wife's condition can be gleaned from her conversations with him or what the doctor tells them during their periodic checkups. Your friend is mystified as to why his wife is upset with him for being "unsupportive." You leave that lunch a little puzzled about your friend's inability to take his wife's perspective. If you have a child with ADD why would you not want to know everything you can about his or her condition? If you do not take time to understand your child's needs are you really invested in his or her future? Take some time to research ADD and in that process you will learn more about a condition that directly affects your entire family. In doing some reading about ADD you can learn things that may improve the welfare of your whole family. This research also demonstrates good faith and your love & concern for your child with ADD. Remember, other people judge us not on our intentions but rather on our actions.

18. **My wife and I frequently find ourselves arguing about things that really relate back to our child with ADD—is this normal?** Couples will argue. People who love one another and live together do not always exist in a rose garden of joy. However, having a child with a disability adds an extra layer of stress in a family and a relationship. Because of your child's disability you will probably face more stress than parents of youngsters who sail through school without many complications. This additional stress may well lead to more arguments and bouts of irritation that directly or indirectly flow out of anxiety caused by your child's condition. Also, there can be some "blame game" that takes place as both spouses try to pin responsibility for their child's disability on one another. In the end, if love exists as a foundation for the relationship, peace will be reestablished. But, if you can stop and realize that your fights and discord are the result of the frustration you feel concerning your child's needs you can break that conflict cycle. There is no way to trace back the direct cause of ADD so any "blame game" is nothing but destructive. The more you and your spouse fight about your child, the more dysfunctional your entire family becomes. Think what effect your fighting has upon your child with ADD and your other children. Do your arguments impact how his or her siblings see your child with ADD? Families are complicated and interconnected systems that can either greatly improve or limit the capacities of their individual members. Identify the source of your arguments and take positive action to deal with those causes instead of engaging in endless and destructive battles.

19. **Will it ever be possible for my child with ADD to hold a job and lead a productive life?** There are many success stories available that spring from the lives of people with ADD. If you

watch a great stand up comedian you are probably observing the actions of a person with ADD. People in the business sector who have to juggle twenty different things at one time while still staying on top of things certainly have a hyperactive tendency. Individuals like Bruce Jenner the Olympic decathlon gold medal winner who is a self-admitted person with ADD who has led a successful & prosperous life, are examples worthy of notice. The writers of this booklet both manifest tendencies that are either ADD or similar in nature. You can succeed in life despite being ADD. In fact, if appropriately directed, the high-energy nature of ADD can be a benefit if the person is in the right field. Key factors for parents and people with ADD to bear in mind are:

a. Find personal strengths.

b. Take steps to encourage and develop those strengths & interests.

c. Make sure the child is exposed to potential careers that match his or her strengths.

d. Provide an encouraging and safe home environment so positive self-esteem evolves.

e. Work with your child to improve social and interpersonal skills.

f. Create opportunities for your child to succeed.

g. Support positive treatment interventions for your child's ADD.

h. Help your child to recognize, accept, and own his or her disability so they can compensate for or harness it.

20. **Will there ever be a time when my child won't need so much of my help?** Being a parent is a livelong job. There is no "retirement" from parenthood short of death. Therefore, your children will need you so long as you are alive. However, the level and type of need they will have for you should change over time. Remember, the better you are at acknowledging, supporting, and helping treat your child's ADD when they are young, the better they will be at demonstrating independence when they grow up. Therein rests the key to this entire process so it is worthy of repetition. If you help treat your child's ADD in an effective and positive way when they are a child and adolescent, the better equipped they will be to become independent and productive adults operating on their own. Like so much of parenting, the influence we exert when children are under our care affects them for the rest of their lives. Make sure that the influence you have on your child's life is positive, nurturing, and loving. If so, you have done all you can to help the child of your heart, mind, and body to be happy. Is that not the goal of every decent parent?

11.

Resources & Links

In your efforts to help your child with ADD blossom it may be beneficial for you to seek out additional information, resources, and links that support that goal. What follows is a sampling of some of these types of resources and supports that you could tap into. Hopefully some of these can serve your family's needs or direct you to other information of benefit.

1. **Children and Adults with Hyperactivity/Attention Deficit Disorder (CHADD):** CHADD remains the most all-encompassing and well known organization specifically focused on the needs of children and adults with ADD. CHADD is an international organization that maintains a comprehensive website, local chapters, and a wide range of supports and resources. CHADD is an organization that can either help you or be a source of information & contacts that may be beneficial to you and your family. CHADD can be contacted either via their website, by mail, or telephone. Contact information is listed below as well as a sample of the web links CHADD"s Internet site can provide. In this case the links are ones focused on educational resources but there are also links for areas such as medical, disability, parent support, and other critical domains.

CHADD National Office
8181 Professional Place - Suite 150
Landover, MD 20785
Tel: 301-306-7070 / Fax: 301-306-7090
http://www.chadd.org/webpage.cfm?cat_id=2&subcat_id=8

CHADD EDUCATIONAL LINKS

American Association of People with Disabilities
URL: http://www.aapd.com/
Description: We're a non-profit, non-partisan, cross-disability organization whose goals are unity, leadership and impact.

Council for Exceptional Children
URL: http://www.cec.sped.org
Description: The Council for Exceptional Children (CEC) is the largest international professional organization dedicated to improving educational outcomes for individuals with exceptionalities, students with disabilities, and/or the gifted.

Council of Parent Attorneys and Advocates
URL: http://www.copaa.net
Description: The prime objective is to better integrate the unique strengths of parent, advocate and attorney to keep the costs of legal assistance manageable, while improving their availability and quality.

ERIC Clearinghouse on Disabilities and Gifted Education

URL: http://www.ericec.org

Description: ERIC EC gathers and disseminates the professional literature, information, and resources on the education and development of individuals of all ages who have disabilities and/or who are gifted.

Families & Advocates Partnership for Education

URL: http://www.fape.org

Description: The Partnership is a new project which aims to inform and educate families and advocates about the Individuals with Disabilities Education Act of 1997 and promising practices.

Federal Resource Center for Special Education

URL: http://www.dssc.org/frc

Description: The FRC supports a nationwide technical assistance network to respond to the needs of students with disabilities, especially students from under-represented populations.

FinAid

URL: http://www.finaid.org/

Description: FinAid was established in the fall of 1994 as a public service. This award-winning site has grown into the most comprehensive annotated collection of information about student financial aid on the web.

Heath Resource Center

URL: http://www.heath.gwu.edu/

Description: The HEATH Resource Center of the American Council on Education is the national clearinghouse on postsecondary education for individuals with disabilities

Misunderstood Minds

URL: http://www.pbs.org/wgbh/misunderstoodminds/

Description: A companion site to the PBS special on learning differences and disabilities. Explore stories from the show and find information and resources for parents

National Association of Private Schools for Exceptional Children

URL: http://www.napsec.com

Description: The National Association of Private Special Education Centers (NAPSEC) is a non-profit association whose mission is to represent private special education programs and affiliated state associations and to ensure access for individuals to appropriate private special education programs and services as vital components of the special education continuum. The association consists of private early intervention services, schools, residential therapeutic centers, and adult living programs that serve both privately and publicly placed individuals with disabilities.

National Association of School Psychologists

URL: http://www.nasponline.org/index2.html

Description: The mission of the National Association of

School Psychologists (NASP) is to promote educationally and psychologically healthy environments for all children and youth by implementing research-based, effective programs that prevent problems, enhance independence, and promote optimal learning. This is accomplished through state-of-the-art research and training, advocacy, ongoing program evaluation, and caring professional service.

National Clearinghouse on Post Secondary Education for Individuals with Disabilities-HEALTH Resource Center
URL: http://www.acenet.edu/
Description: ACE is dedicated to the belief that equal educational opportunity and a strong higher education system are essential cornerstones of a democratic society.

Pacer Center
URL: http://www.pacer.org
Description: The mission of PACER Center is to expand opportunities and enhance the quality of life of children and young adults with disabilities and their families, based on the concept of parents helping parents.

Link: University of California Los Angeles Center for Neurobehavioral Genetics Attention Deficit Hyperactivity Disorder
URL: http://www.adhd.ucla.edu
Description: This website was created by the research team currently conducting several NIH funded studies to identify risk genes underlying ADHD. The website summarizes our current understanding of the genetics of

ADHD and describes opportunities for families to help further that understanding by becoming participants in research.

2. **Wrights Law:** This website is among the best in terms of parental rights and information about schools and the legal requirements related to ADD and other disabilities. The website maintains a number of sections inclusive of an excellent one dealing specifically with ADD. This is a user friendly site that includes articles, resources, links, tips, legislative updates, FAQ's, and a Q&A section. It can be found on the Internet at: http://www.wrightslaw.com/

3. **Selected Readings:** While there are many books available to parents about raising a child with ADD here is a sampling of recommended readings drawn from the CHADD online bookstore:

- **Understanding Girls with Attention Deficit Hyperactivity Disorder**
  Kathleen G. Nadeau, Ph.D. Patricia O. Quinn, Ellen Littman

  A groundbreaking book for parents, health care professionals and educators, designed to increase awareness of girls with AD/HD. Specifically targets each developmental and educational stage - from toddler years through adolescence.

- **Teenagers with ADD: A Parents' Guide**
  Chris A. Ziegler Dendy, M.S.

  Parents, educators, and healthcare professionals rely on this best-selling book to understand and cope with teenagers with ADD and ADHD. This guide offers comprehensive treatment of the special issues and challenges faced by families and professionals including diagnosis and treatment, academic problems, legal issues and planning for life after high school graduation.

- **The ADHD Book of Lists: A Practical Guide for Helping Children and Teens with Attention Deficit Disorders Sandra Rief**

  The AD/HD Book of lists is a comprehensive, reliable source of answers, practical strategies, and tools in a convenient list format. Created for teachers, parents, school psychologists, medical and mental health professionals, counselors, and other school personnel, this important resource contains the most current information about AD/HD. It is filled with strategies, supports and interventions that have been found to be the most effective in minimizing the problems and optimizing the success of children and teens with ADHD.

- **Maybe You Know My Teen: A Parent's Guide to Helping Your Adolescent With Attention Deficit Hyperactivity Disorder Mary Fowler**

  Adolescence is a tumultuous turning point for everyone, but for teens with ADHD and their parents, it can be especially challenging. Both may find more conflict over home issues. Predictably there's a lot of stress over inconsistent or poor school performance and over inevitable decisions regarding higher education and life after high school.

  Maybe You Know My Teen offers hope and help to parents struggling with the more complex issues of raising an adolescent with the disorder. It brims with management strategies for parents new to ADHD as well as those who have coped with it throughout their child's life Explaining the roots of the disorder clearly and extensively, while discussing situations most likely to cause symptoms to manifest themselves, Mary Fowler presents step-by-step advice, along with in-depth personal stories and first-person advice from the leading experts in the field. Dr. Barkley deems it, "Unequivocally, the best book that has ever been available for parents of an adolescent with ADHD."

- **From Chaos to Calm: Effective Parenting for Challenging Children with ADHD and Other Behavioral Problems**

  Janet E. Heininger, Ph.D., and Sharon K. Weiss, M.Ed.

  Foreword by Sam Goldstein, Ph.D., coauthor of Raising Resilient Children

  This fascinating new book provides unique perspectives and helpful suggestions for parents of challenging children including:

  - Establishing daily routines
  - Setting realistic goals
  - Learning to deal with stalling, forgetting, overreacting and other behavioral problems
  - Working with teachers and finding professional help when needed
  - Engaging in proactive, not reactive, parenting
  - Avoiding common traps and pitfalls when dealing with a challenging child
  - Teaching important skills

- **ADHD: A Survival Guide for Parents and Teachers**

  Richard A. Lougy, M.F.T. and David K. Rosenthal, M.D.

  ADHD A Survival Guide for Parents and teachers addresses issues and concerns confronting parents and teachers who raise and teach AD/HD children. The friendly and supportive style of the book is easy to understand and use. Parents and teachers will appreciate the sympathetic approach and expert discussion by authors who have worked extensively with ADHD children and their families in a broad range of settings, including medical, clinical and educational.

- **Wrightslaw: From Emotions to Advocacy: The Special Education Survival Guide**

  Pete and Pam Wright

  Are you beginning to advocate for a child with a disability? Are you an experienced advocate who needs a good reference book? Do you feel confused about how to advocate for a child with a disability?

  In this comprehensive, easy-to-read book, you learn to:

  - Develop a master plan for your child's special education
  - Organize you child's life
  - Work with consultants
  - Write SMART IEP goals and objectives
  - Use test scores to monitor your child's progress
  - Resolve parent-school conflict early
  - Write effective letters & create paper trails
  - Use parent agendas to improve meeting outcomes.

- **Why Johnny Doesn't Behave: Twenty Tips for Measurable BIPs**

  Barbara Bateman and Annemieke Golly

  Why Johnny Doesn't Behave focuses on 20 concrete tips to help you write measurable behavioral goals and objectives. Tips include; making clear classroom expectations; directing teaching expectations; minimizing attention to minor inappropriate behaviors and paying attention to behavior you want. Clear direction is given so you can achieve these basic goals. The final section is devoted to Functional Behavior Assessments (FBAs) and Behavioral Intervention Plans (BIPs). It begins with a lucid explanation of each and ends with sample FBA's and BIP's so you can see how to write your own.

- **A Bird's-Eye View of Life with ADD and ADHD: Advice from Young Survivors**

  Chris A. Ziegler Dendy, M.S., Alex Ziegler

  At last, a book for teenagers and preteens filled with great advice from young people who are living with ADHD. Through humor and personal examples, these young survivors give advice on disorganization, sleep problems, forgetfulness, medication, and much more. Since teens are more likely to listen to other teens than adults, this book is the perfect educational tool.

- **School Strategies for ADD Teens**

  Kathleen Nadeau

  This well-organized book outlines how to get the help you need in high school for your AD/HD teen, including I.E.P. development, accommodations, and management strategies.

- **Teaching Teens with ADD and ADHD: A Quick Reference Guide for Teachers and Parents**

  Chris A. Ziegler-Dendy, M.S.

  This detailed companion guide to Teenagers with ADD offers parents, teachers and other professionals 75 concise summaries aimed at ensuring school success for students with ADD/ADHD. This comprehensive guide provides effective interventions strategies for key academic issues including common learning problems, executive function deficits, IDEA & Section 504, development of IEP's and 504 plans, Functional Behavior Assessment and Behavior Intervention Plans, classroom management, and medication.

- **Raise Your Child's Social IQ : Stepping Stones to People Skills for Kids**

  Cathi Cohen, L.C.S.W.

  Some children are born with good social instincts, but many children are not. This very practical, step-by-step plan outlines a customized program that can be taught at home by parents, and is also appropriate at school for use by school counselors.

- **Making the System Work for Your Child with ADHD**

  Peter S. Jensen, M.D.

  Even for parents who "do everything right," the road to successful management of ADHD is seldom smooth. Now leading child psychiatrist Dr. Peter Jensen guides parents over the rough patches and around the hairpin curves in this empowering, highly informative book. Readers learn the "whats," "whys," and "how-tos" of making the system work-getting their money's worth from the healthcare system, cutting through red tape at school, and making the most of fleeting time with doctors and therapists.

- **Straight Talk about Psychological Testing for Kids**
  Ellen Braaten, Ph.D., and Gretchen Felopulos, Ph.D.

  With nearly 20 years of combined experience in the field, Dr. Ellen Braaten and Dr. Gretchen Felopulos explain the role testing plays in diagnosing and devising treatment plans for dyslexia, ADHD, math and reading disorders, and other childhood problems, including Asperger syndrome, depression, and anxiety. You'll learn what to expect as testing unfolds, how to crack the code of numerical scores and jargon-filled reports, ways to make the process less stressful for children, and what your options are each step of the way.

- **Freeing Your Child from Anxiety: Powerful, Practical Solutions to Overcome Your Child's Fears, Worries, and Phobias**
  Tamar E. Chansky, Ph.D.

  In Freeing Your Child From Anxiety, a childhood anxiety disorder specialist examines all manifestations of childhood fears, including social anxiety, Tourette's Syndrome, hair-pulling, and Obsessive Compulsive Disorder, and guides you through a proven program to help your child back to emotional safety.

- **Helping Children Learn: Intervention Handouts for School and Home**

  Jack A. Naglieri, Ph.D. and Eric B.

  This guide offers a fresh approach to teaching children who struggle in school. Featuring almost 50 intervention handouts that really help children learn, the book is ideal for teachers to use in the classroom and for parents to use at home. School psychologists can use the short questionnaire based on Naglieri & Das's Cognitive Assessment System to assess student strengths and needs and help direct interventions.

- **Helping Your Teenager Beat Depression: A Problem-Solving Approach for Families**

  Katharina Manassis, M.D., FRCPC, and Anne Marie Levac, R.N., MN

  Helping Your Teenager Beat Depression presents the authors' unique strategy that enables parents to become effective partners in the treatment of their child's depression. Whether their teen is withdrawn, sad, angry, or anxious, parents can immediately begin to help their child and themselves by using the L.E.A.P. program, a problem-solving strategy based on cognitive-behavioral therapy, a widely-recognized and proven treatment.

- **When Moms and Kids Have ADD**

  Patricia O. Quinn, M.D.

  Rather than offering parenting advice that may be highly unrealistic, this book starts by addressing a mothers needs, helping her to understand the importance of getting help for herself before she can succeed in helping her kids.

Author's Bookstore

Copies of ADD 101: A Parent's Resource Guide can be ordered as E-books via our website. In addition Mr. Romaneck has several other books available either via commercial Internet sites such as Amazon, Borders, & Barnes and Noble or in the form of E-books. Listed below are some other publications that Mr. Romaneck has available. While these do not specifically deal with ADD they do offer insights into self-improvement, personal growth, communication, and inner qualities needed to successfully face the difficulties sometimes confronted in life.

A Superior Journey:

Trail Reflections from Isle Royale: In this chronicle of a 200-mile backpacking trip in a remote Northwoods park the author deals with issues not only of wilderness but also loss, self-improvement, and discovery.

Prairie Musings:

A selection of poems drawn from the external and inner landscapes of Illinois.

Leadership in Schools:

A sampling of practical suggestions for parents and educators for coping with many of the pressures and issues attendant to schools. Topics include areas such as coping with depression, dealing with anxiety, burn out, ethical behavior, and communication.

E-BOOKS
(AVAILABLE DIRECTLY FORM THE AUTHOR):

1. Lincoln & Leadership:

100 of President Lincoln's most heartfelt sayings with an accompanying reflective essay by the author. Each selection deals with subjects such as crisis management, trust, reputation, compassion, and understanding. Cost = $5.00

2. The Middle Way of Childhood:

Readers are provided with 150 Buddhist sayings drawn from the classics of this ancient philosophical system. Each saying is accompanied by a reflective writing centering on how to better work with, love, and support children. Cost = $5.00

3. Tao for the Day:

A daybook of Taoist sayings and reflections. 365 quotations taken from major Taoist works each of which is accompanied by a reflective thought for the day. This work taps into the ancient Chinese philosophy that emphasized balance and perspective in our daily lives. Cost = $5.00

To order E-books simply contact the author
at the address or email address listed below.
Then send a check, money order, or cash payment to:

GREG M. ROMANECK
613 FRANKLIN
DeKALB, IL 60115

gregromaneck@hotmail.com

ONE STUDENT

Arriving in my classroom I nervously look out of the corners of my eyes.

I long to be accepted—to have friends—to feel safe.

I am different, but so is everyone.

I am the child who stands out in ways that seem obscure.

When I try to read words & letters squirm like silver fish caught in a net.

The words I write scratch their way across the page like earthworms in the yard after a rain.

If asked a question my mind flip-flops like a fox caught in a trap.

I know the answer to question 3 when the class is on number 5.

There are times when I act out—and I really don't know why.

Sometimes people—even my parents—think I'm lazy.

But I know that I try; and try; and try—oh so hard!

I know what I know and what I don't.

The class moves so fast and sometimes I feel like I'm stuck in the mud.

Yet, despite these truths, I want to be someone—a policeman, fireman, or a teacher.

I know I'll need help to get "smarter".

On the hardest days—when my brain feels like a dull pencil dragging along—I want to quit.

Please don't let me quit—I have so much inside of me.

About the Authors:

Both Derek Harkema and Greg M. Romaneck have been working with children, adolescents, and families for many decades. In those years both of these professionals have dedicated many hours to the task of helping youngsters with ADHD and their families to better cope with the needs that are manifest within this condition. In addition, both Mr. Harkema & Mr. Romaneck have had direct familial experience with the nature of ADHD. Professionally, Derek Harkema has worked as a clinical social worker, therapist, advocate, and consultant in a broad range of therapeutic domains. Mr. Romaneck has served as a professional educator with extensive experience as a special education teacher, supervisor, and director. At present Mr. Harkema is working as a private consultant and therapist in Seattle, Washington. Mr. Romaneck is serving as the Director of Human Resources for the Batavia School District #101 in Batavia, IL. While this is the first formal publication the authors have undertaken together it is far from their first collaboration. In addition, Mr. Harkema has conducted training sessions not only on ADHD but many other therapeutic topics in venues such as correctional institutions, universities, educational institutions, and many other related fields. Mr. Romaneck is an avid writer who has published over 170 articles, seven books, and over 1200 children's book reviews. In his spare time Mr. Harkema enjoys racecars, the out of doors, travel, and Internet commerce. Mr.

Romaneck takes time to go on wilderness backpacking excursions, cross country bicycling, reading, writing, gardening, and spending time with his family and friends.

www.ingramcontent.com/pod-product-compliance
Lightning Source LLC
Chambersburg PA
CBHW020247290526
45784CB00003B/1137